THE GARDENER'S WEED BOOK

Earth-Safe Controls

Barbara Pleasant

Illustrated by Regina Hughes
and Bobbi Angell

A Down-to-Earth Gardening Book from Storey Publishing

STOREY

STOREY COMMUNICATIONS, INC.
SCHOOLHOUSE ROAD
POWNAL, VERMONT 05261

*The mission of Storey Communications is to serve our customers
by publishing practical information that encourages personal independence
in harmony with the environment.*

Edited by Pamela Lappies
Technical review by Larry W. Mitich, Ph.D.
Cover and text design by Cynthia McFarland
Text production by Cynthia McFarland and Susan Bernier
Indexed by Northwind Editorial Services

Printed in the United States by R.R. Donnelley

10 9 8 7 6 5 4 3 2 1

Library of Congress Cataloging-in-Publication Data

Pleasant, Barbara.
   The gardener's weed book : earth-safe controls / Barbara Pleasant
   p.   cm.
   Includes bibliographical references and index.
   ISBN 0-88266-921-4 (pbk. : alk. paper)
   1. Weeds — Control — North America.   2. Weeds — North America —
      Identification.   I. Title.
SB611.P55   1996
635'.04958—dc20   95-48408
                                                                CIP

635.04958
PLE

Creeping buttercup

Contents

Acknowledgments

I would like to thank Dr. Larry W. Mitich of the University of California for making weeds intriguing and for his tolerance of my non-technical language during his technical review of this book. Painstaking research done by dozens of other weed scientists, botanists, and ecologists enriches these pages. On behalf of myself and other weed-challenged gardeners, thank you one and all.

Words are only one part of this book. Original drawings by Bobbi Angel brought greenbrier and other garden weeds to life, and completed the impeccable collection of drawings done 25 years ago by Regina O. Hughes. Pictures such as these are worth thousands of words.

About the Illustrator

Regina Olson Hughes was born in Herman, Nebraska, on February 1, 1895, to parents who left Wisconsin in a covered wagon long before Nebraska became a state. Her family encouraged her artistic talent and sent her to art school in Omaha.

Upon graduating from Gallaudet College for the Deaf in Washington, D.C. in 1918, Hughes earned a Master's Degree in 1920. During World War I she worked as a translator for the State Department, then at the War and Commerce Departments. She married Gallaudet professor Dr. Frederick Hughes in 1923 and in 1930 went to work at the United States Department of Agriculture, first as a research clerk and later as a scientific illustrator.

Awarded the USDA's Superior Service Award for botanical illustration and technical translation in 1962, Hughes received an Honorary Doctorate of Humane Letters from Gallaudet in 1967. She retired from USDA in 1969 and started a second career working at the Smithsonian Institution, painting orchids and bromeliads for Dr. Robert Read and continuing to illustrate for USDA scientists.

Her most prominent works include *Selected Weeds of the United States*, a USDA Handbook published in 1969 which has been reprinted by Dover Books, and *Economically Important Foreign Weeds: Potential Problems in the United States*, containing 6,000 of her drawings along with descriptions of the plants written by her.

Regina Hughes died at her home in Washington, D.C., on August 12 in 1993.

CHAPTER 1

THE
WIDE WORLD
OF WEEDS

THIS BOOK IS about the plants gardeners love to hate, which we call weeds. Through the ages, people have attempted to define weeds, always with inadequate results. Are they "plants whose virtues have yet to be discovered" (Walt Whitman), "guardians of the soil" (Joseph Cocannouer), or something equally nice, or are they sly thieves who steal the soil's resources and gardeners' precious time?

All of the above! During the months that I have been writing this book, summer has arrived, and with it have come bounteous crops of weeds. Although my yard is only average in size, I have accumulated a small mountain of weeds that are now piled high in the deep shade beyond my compost heap. Many of them were attempting to fulfill the honorable mission of healing over soil that I had left open and scarred, but others had no rightful claim to be where I found them. In the sweaty company of these rowdy wild plants, I decided that weeds can only be defined from a practical point of view: weeds are any plants that insist on growing where you don't want them to grow.

It so happens that the same plants trespass into gardens time after time. This book encompasses 80 weeds that are commonly found in North

American *gardens* — not necessarily fields, meadows, pastures, or roadside ditches. True *garden* weeds are special, for they thrive on the constant change that takes place in gardens as we plant and replant our beds, borders, and rows.

Many wild plants that are technically classified as weeds cannot tolerate the continual shifting about that we gardeners do, so it's more fitting to regard them as wildflowers rather than garden weeds. Some examples include wild asters, daisies, ironweeds, goldenrods, and sunflowers. Rarely will you catch these roadside weeds trying to crowd out your tomatoes or attempting to steal nutrients from the soil you prepared for your lilies.

These dastardly deeds are done by what I call garden weeds — plants like crabgrass, redroot pigweed, lambsquarters, and the many others that are described in detail in Chapters 3, 4, and 5. We tend to think of weeds as superplants since they do such a great job of invading our gardens, but in reality weeds can only thrive where we make a place for them. Most garden weeds absolutely depend on humans to provide them with an open place to grow, and they further benefit from our efforts to keep soil fertile and moist. Where humans cultivate, garden weeds grow.

WHY WEEDS?

Ecologically speaking, most garden weeds are weaklings in the long run. They do a terrible job of adapting to established natural ecosystems (like a mature forest or grassy prairie). If you were to abandon your garden tomorrow and let nature have its way with the place, most plants that fit into the category of *garden* weeds would be gone within a few years. In fact, you might think of garden weeds as the emergency squad that shows up to put things right when we gardeners begin wielding our shovels to create the artificial ecosystems that we call gardens.

Garden weeds are experts at colonizing disturbed soil, which is exactly what a garden is to a weed: a space where the earth has been opened up like a wound that must be healed. For this much, weeds must be respected. Weeds, in turn, have no respect for a gardener's goal of enriching land with beautiful, fragrant, delicious, and otherwise useful plants. Yet the missions of gardeners and the objectives of weeds often are the same: to bring stability to disturbed sites so that those places can regain their lost function in Nature's wild scheme. Weeds just go about things differently than we do.

The Weed Seed Bonanza

Take seeds, for example. When we gardeners plant seeds, we operate within countable numbers — say 25 seeds for a planting of squash or a few hundred for a nice row of zinnias or beans. But most garden weeds produce so many seeds that it's small exaggeration to call their version of seed production a *seed rain*. In a good year, a healthy crabgrass plant can drop 100,000 seeds, and lambsquarters can beat that number five times over. Along with amazing numbers, weed seeds (and the roots of tenacious perennial weeds) have an almost supernatural gift of longevity. For example, if you were to bury a bunch of assorted weed seeds a foot deep and leave them there for five years, when you finally brought them to the surface, you could expect about 25 percent of them to sprout. Try the same experiment with seeds of cultivated onion or lettuce, and germination will be zero.

Managing Your Garden's Bank Account

All gardeners can assume that every square inch of their garden soil contains weed seeds. Some of them may have been there for years, while some dropped or blew in only yesterday. The seeds that exist naturally in any soil are called the soil's seed bank. And just as with the dollars in your checking account, repeated withdrawals will make the balance go down. If no deposits are made (by allowing weeds to drop seeds or importing weed-seed bearing manure or topsoil, for example), you can make your balance go lower and lower — maybe by as much as 25 percent a year in the first three years. But you will never bankrupt your soil's weed seed bank, for some seeds will always blow in or perhaps hitch a ride on the feet of a passing bird.

To drive the balance in your soil's weed seed bank close to bankruptcy, the most important thing to do is to prevent weeds from shedding their seeds. Where weeds are allowed to grow and reproduce freely, about 95 percent of the weed seeds in the bank come from weeds that dropped seed in previous seasons.

Solar-Powered Weeds

Many weed seeds are extremely tiny. All seeds contain food energy that the new sprout uses for its initial growth, and the tinier the seed, the fewer food reserves the plants have to sustain them during and just after germination.

So how do plants that are handicapped by minuscule seed size survive? They take the energy they need from the sun, that's how.

This simple explanation of how tiny weed seeds manage to survive so well can be used to your advantage in your garden. Since many common weeds that sprout from little seeds absolutely must have light to germinate and grow, controlling the amount of light that hits the soil can help control weeds.

There are several ways to deny weed seeds the light they so desperately need. One strategy is to avoid constantly turning up the soil so that new weed seeds (which were previously buried) are close enough to sunlight to take advantage of its energy. Sunshine cannot help seeds that are buried more than an inch deep, so hoeing or cultivating only the very top of your soil will result in fewer weed seeds germinating than if you were to go deeper, and thereby drag weed seeds up into the "germination zone."

Mulching exposed soil also limits the life-giving sunshine small-seeded weeds need, as does maintaining a thick canopy of foliage over the soil. Scientists have found that one of the reasons fewer weeds emerge from soil that is partially shaded by plants is that a foliage canopy changes the type of light that filters through. In other words, it's not just weed *plants* that are set back by shade; many weed *seeds* require bright, unfiltered light to trigger germination.

The Myth of Weedy Manure

Some gardeners are reluctant to use manure to enrich their soil for fear that it contains many weed seeds. Yet the number of weed seeds in manure depends on what the animals eat and can be very high or close to nothing. When manure seeds were counted in 60 cow manure samples taken from 20 farms in New York, manure from four of the farms contained no weed seeds at all. Most of the others showed a broad array of weed seeds, with lambsquarters, chickweed, dandelion, and mustard among the most common. The only truly noxious seed found in any of the samples was velvetleaf, which showed up in the manure from one farm.

As long as the animals that produce the manure you put in your garden do not subsist on weeds, you can use the manure with confidence to improve your soil's structure and fertility. Also keep in mind that it's easier to control weeds than to grow plants in weak, infertile soil.

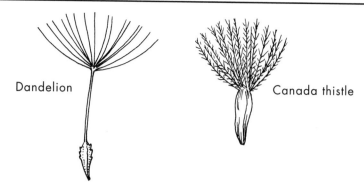

Dandelion

Canada thistle

Most weed seeds are equipped either to travel or to stay put, whichever serves them best. Dandelion and Canada thistle blow about with the help of their downy parachutes.

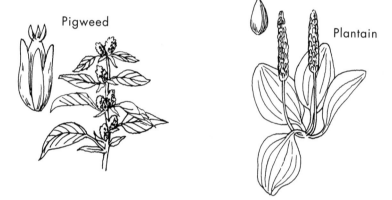

Pigweed

Plantain

Pigweed and plantain have smooth surfaces and shapes that help them slip into soil crevices.

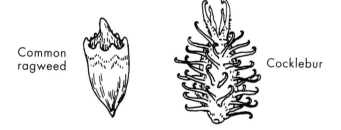

Common ragweed

Cocklebur

Ragweed and cocklebur sink their hooks into passing animals to help them find new homes.

The Wide World of Weeds

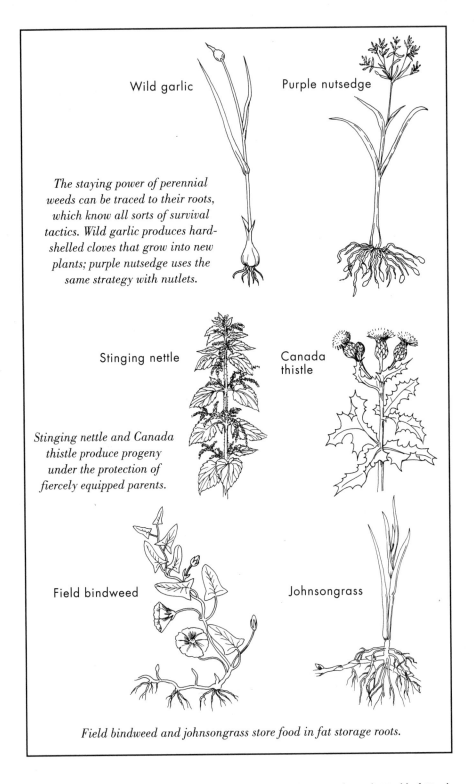

Wild garlic

Purple nutsedge

The staying power of perennial weeds can be traced to their roots, which know all sorts of survival tactics. Wild garlic produces hard-shelled cloves that grow into new plants; purple nutsedge uses the same strategy with nutlets.

Stinging nettle

Canada thistle

Stinging nettle and Canada thistle produce progeny under the protection of fiercely equipped parents.

Field bindweed

Johnsongrass

Field bindweed and johnsongrass store food in fat storage roots.

The Wide World of Weeds

The constant shade of nearby plants also may keep some weed seeds from germinating by limiting the changes in soil temperature at different times of day. The daytime warming and nighttime cooling that takes place in open soil encourages the germination of some weed seeds. Shade decreases those temperature changes, which also helps reduce the number of weed seeds that come to life.

Listening to Your Weeds

One of the confusing aspects of garden weeds has to do with the types of soil in which they grow best. Some people think weeds have a lot to tell them about their soil's fertility, moisture level, and pH, when actually weeds reveal little about such important matters. For example, it is often said that the appearance of sorrel indicates poor, acidic soil, when the truth is that sorrel *will grow* in poor acidic soil. But it will also grow in fertile, neutral soil! A soil test is much more trustworthy than any weed.

Yet it is true that you can tell a few things about your soil by studying your weeds. Two trends to watch for are:

■ Crabgrass, annual bluegrass, Carolina geranium, and plantain will grow in very acidic soil with a pH of 4.8. Slightly acidic soil with a pH of 5.2 is acceptable to jimsonweed and tall morningglory. If these are predominant weeds in your soil, don't be surprised if a pH test indicates that you should add lime to bring your soil into the normal range.

■ Redroot pigweed, chickweed, dandelion, and wild mustard appear pale and stunted when grown in acidic soils. For them, a near neutral pH of 5.8 to 6.0 (the same level preferred by most crop plants) is necessary for lush, rampant growth. As long as these weeds are growing beautifully, you can feel more confident about your soil's acid balance.

As proof that weeds are often poor indicators, take an honest look at your weed community. In spring, do you see plantain, chickweed, and crabgrass growing side by side? In summer, is morningglory scrambling up your pigweed? The weeds in your garden do have stories to tell about the spot's history and seed bank, but you can do a much better job than they when it comes to evaluating the quality of your soil.

UNDERGROUND WEEDS

New annual weeds usually sprout from seeds, but hardy perennial weeds have other ways of making sure they stay alive. True, long-lived perennial weeds like bindweed and johnsongrass produce seeds, but they're usually small or relatively few in number. Instead, many perennial weeds reproduce vegetatively, without flowers and seeds, or by producing seeds as an after-thought. For example, new quackgrass plants can sprout from bits of root; nutsedge and wild garlic grow from bulblets left behind in the soil when the mother weed is pulled; and bermuda and johnsongrass sprout from pieces of rhizome (a sort of a stem-root structure) that become brittle and break off when you try to dig out the plants.

These vegetative plant parts often succeed at reproduction where seeds fail since they contain substantial food reserves to help tide the new plant over until it's ready to stand on its own. Most of the weeds capable of multiplying by spreading vegetatively *and* by making seeds take care of first things first: they develop above-ground runners or underground buds (or rhizomes or corms) *before* they attempt to flower.

Keep this in mind when managing weeds that spread into colonies. Although you might wait until flower buds form on annual weeds to chop them down, attack spreading perennials early and often to make sure you don't work any harder than you really need to.

THE WEEDY ADVANTAGE

Weeds find much of their strength in numbers, which is the main strategy they use to take over your garden. Yet many weeds are also masters of time and opportunity. They seem to know exactly when to grow, and amaze and frustrate us with their success.

The most successful weeds are closely keyed to the cultural sequence of certain crops, almost as if they are natural partners. For example, the pretty flower called bachelor's button *(Centaurea cyanus)* joined the ranks of weeds in Europe 300 years ago (and more recently in the Pacific North-west) since it did so well when grown in winter wheat. Bachelor's buttons like everything about winter wheat — the time it is planted, the soil in which it grows, and also the way it is harvested. The seeds even blend right in with wheat berries! Before such things were clearly understood, supersti-tious seventeenth-century farmers thought evil spirits could turn grain into "hurt-sickle."

From Mimicry to Cross-Breeding

There have been cases in which weeds and closely related cultivated crops grew alongside one another, flowered at the same
time, cross-pollinated, and hybridized themselves into superweeds.
This has occurred with beets, radishes, and sorghum. Unfortunately, the most glaring difference between the superweed and its
cultivated counterpart is that the weed is much more adaptable
and is willing to grow in less than perfect conditions. By comparison, the cultivated plant is much less hardy. But the cultivated plant
is the one that's pretty or tastes good, so of course that's the one
we want.

Scientists call this near perfect fit between weeds and cultivated plants
crop mimicry. Barnyardgrass is now a common weed in many different
crops, but it got its big break by partnering up with rice. Weedy nightshades
have flourished in many areas when they sneaked into the cropping systems
of their cousin, the tomato, and wild mustards made a similar move into
fields planted with cabbage.

Perhaps you've seen mimicry at work in your garden when you thought
you were growing a wonderful tower of pole beans, only to find morningglory
vines overpowering your beans one day. Get to know any and all resident
weeds that have this trick up their sleeve and focus your control efforts on
them before they bamboozle you.

WEED-TO-PLANT WARFARE

Besides great timing, weeds use other strategies to assure themselves of
long, prosperous lives. Their big thing is competition. The most successful
weeds grow so fast that they have no trouble stealing the space, light,
nutrients, and water that we had hoped would go to our lettuce. Crabgrass,
one of the fastest growing plants on the planet, is a prime example.

Some weeds are downright detrimental to other plants, and have been
designed by nature to turn the garden into their own little kingdom. They
exude chemicals from their roots that act as poison to other plants, or
perhaps they "sabotage" the site in other ways. Nutsedge hosts soil-
dwelling bacteria that destroy soil-borne nitrogen, the most important
nutrient for most growing plants. Bermudagrass roots give off chemicals that
slow the growth of other plants, even peach trees! This plant-to-plant

chemical warfare is called allelopathy, and weeds are well equipped to fight their own battles for space.

Allelopathy is not a new idea, at least where weeds are concerned. The Greek philosopher Democritus noted it in the fifth century BC, and 200 years later Theophrastus puzzled over why some plants inhibit the growth of others after setting aside the usual factors of competition for light, nutrients, and water. In 1937, this ability of plants to interfere with the growth of their neighbors was finally given a name: allelopathy.

Several weeds provide textbook cases of allelopathy in action. When lambsquarters starts flowering, the roots release toxic levels of oxalic acid into the soil. Velvetleaf carries toxic substances on its leaves, which rain washes into the soil. Scientists are now confident in saying that several weeds — quackgrass, Canada thistle, johnsongrass, giant foxtail, black mustard, and yellow nutsedge, among others — hinder other plants while they are alive, through competition and allelopathy, and after they are dead by releasing plant-killing chemical residues.

Some weeds go even further by enlisting the cooperation of soil-dwelling bacteria in an attempt to keep other plants away from crowding their space. Ragweed, crabgrass, prostrate spurge, and some prairie grasses may be able to counteract the work of rhizobium bacteria, the soil-dwelling microorganisms that help legumes (like peas and beans) fix nitrogen from the air.

Perhaps you've noticed that when gardening conditions get bad — during droughts or plagues of grasshoppers, for instance — weeds tend to fare better than cultivated plants. This edge cannot be credited to allelopathy; you have to look backward in time. Cultivated plants like beans and corn have been selected over hundreds of years to grow in the pampered situation of gardens and cultivated fields, where they are provided with good soil, generous spacing, and supplemental water. Their root systems are only as large as they need to be and in some cases (such as lettuce) may be downright skimpy.

Weeds, on the other hand, have developed very large root systems that may be measured in feet rather than inches as a primary survival strategy. Whereas bean roots may reach down a foot or so, the deepest roots of redroot pigweed grow down three times as far!

This is both good and bad. In light of the primary mission of most garden weeds — to heal over and restore open soil — deep-rooted weeds not only survive but pull nutrients from deep in the subsoil up to the

The Wide World of Weeds

surface. But it's bad news for gardeners, since weeds constantly interfere with the welfare of our plants. All gardens have weeds, and all good gardeners must find ways to get rid of them.

THE WHO'S WHO OF WEEDS

A dozen gardeners in different parts of the country helped me hone down the list of weeds that qualify as *garden* weeds, and I'm confident that most North American gardeners will find most of their weeds in this book. Yet you will probably also encounter weeds that defy easy identification, or weeds that are not supposed to be in your area at all! Weeds have an uncanny knack for moving from place to place unexpectedly, often in very novel ways. Shoe soles, truck tires, aircraft wings, bird's feet, and thousands of other objects may serve as free transportation of weed seeds from one place to another. During the months I have worked on this book, often with a half-dozen weed reference books open on the floor around my desk, I have been unable to identify at least 42 weeds in my own yard.

Identification can be especially challenging within the large weed families, such as the wild mustards, the pigweeds, docks, and all of the grasses. But if you can come close to identifying your common weeds by figuring out their likely family affiliation, you will quickly come to understand the plant and what to do to keep it under control. If you guess the family of a certain weed but are still having trouble pinning down its identity, check the family groups in Chapter 6.

Good methods for controlling weeds are explored in the next chapter, because all gardens have weeds. It's just their nature.

CHAPTER 2

THE BASICS
OF
WEED CONTROL

MOST OF THIS BOOK is about individual weeds — where and how they grow and the best ways to control them. Getting to know the weeds that inhabit your garden space is crucial to reducing their numbers, so you will probably refer to Chapters 3, 4, and 5 — the Galleries of Weeds — again and again.

At the same time, there are a number of strategies and methods to use in managing your overall weed situation, which is the subject of this section. First we'll look at large-scale measures that have a broad impact on all weeds — methods that can shrink the balance in your garden's weed seed bank in a big way. These methods include cover cropping, using smother plants, and mulching. Then we'll look at specific strategies to use to reduce the time you spend fighting weeds, the best tools to use, and what to do with your weeds once you have them in a wheelbarrow or garden cart.

GAINING GROUND WITH COVER CROPS

A cover crop helps control weeds by deceit. Since weeds colonize open, disturbed soil, they are naturally discouraged when the soil is well covered with healthy plant life. Plants that can be used to temporarily or permanently cover arable ground are called cover crops. Some are allowed to grow and are then mowed down or turned under, while others can be used as permanent companions for vegetables and fruits. Either way, cover crops discourage weeds and help improve the soil at the same time.

You need to think through how you intend to use cover crops to make them really work for you. Grain-type covers, such as annual rye, cereal rye, or wheat, produce a huge amount of top growth, and the roots tend to be quite extensive, too. For these reasons, it's impossible to plant a crop *into* an established stand of uncut grain. However, you can allow the grain to grow from fall to spring and then mow it down and allow the stubble to dry where it falls. To plant in this dry mulch, open up small spaces here and there and plant in those open hills. Vine crops such as watermelon, cantaloupe, and sweet potatoes often do very well when grown this way.

Some cover crops grow best during the winter months, flower in spring, and then cease growth through much of the summer, just when you want to use the space to grow vegetables. The best example is subterranean clover *(Trifolium subterraneum)*, a European legume. When sown in fall (and inoculated with nitrogen-fixing bacteria to help it grow strong and fast), subterranean clover becomes a winter cover crop that improves the soil. After flowering in early spring, the fertilized "pegs" establish themselves in the soil for next year's cover crop. Subterranean clover does not grow and spread during the summer months as most other clovers do, so it's an ideal cover crop for places where you will be growing summer crops like corn. In a study done in New Jersey, a cover crop of subterranean clover controlled

Cover Crops and Wide-Row Planting

Many people who grow large gardens plant their crops in wide rows and keep the walkways between the rows in mixed cover crops, such as a mixture of white clover, red clover, and buckwheat. The cover crop rows serve as a habitat for spiders and other beneficial insects, and the clovers help enrich the soil by fixing nitrogen from the air. As long as these between-row stands remain thick, few weeds are able to grow there.

Of course, you don't get habitat for more than a dozen beneficial insects without putting some work into this plan. Depending on rainfall, you will need to mow the cover crop rows (usually about once a month). The clover clippings make excellent mulch, however, and if you use a mower that throws the clipping out a chute on the side, you automatically mulch adjoining crop rows as you mow. To make sure your beneficial insects always have a place to go, try to mow only some of the mixed cover crop rows on a given day, or better yet plan your mowing so that alternating rows are mowed in alternating weeks.

The Basics of Weed Control

morningglory and weedy grasses in corn better than herbicides and slightly increased the corn yield to boot!

You can even use weeds as cover crops provided you turn them under *before* they have a chance to develop viable seeds or mow them so often that flowers never have a chance to develop. For example, let's say that you cleaned out the bed where you grew spring lettuce and three weeks later found a strapping stand of pigweed, lambsquarters, and other weeds in its place. If you let these weeds grow for a few weeks and then turn them under, you can consider that space cover cropped!

STIFLING WEEDS WITH SMOTHER CROPS

You can use *cultivated* plants to smother out unwanted weeds, too. This method consists of sowing a specially selected companion crop that forms a weed-suppressing ground cover beneath your crop plants. The only trick is to provide enough water for both the primary crop and the smother plants.

Scientists are starting work that may result in a new generation of plants specifically designed to work as smother crops, but for now gardeners can think in terms of lettuce, mustard, and other leafy greens, as well as fast-growing bush beans or field peas. None of these is exactly right for the job. Lettuce often sprouts slowly, most leafy greens grow upward instead of outward, and beans and peas eventually get quite tall. Yet you can help with these shortcomings. For example, you might broadcast turnips a week ahead

---

What Is a Smother Crop?

Ideally, a smother crop should have these four characteristics:

Fast sprouting, so it will come up at least as fast as the weeds it's supposed to smother.

Broad leaves that spread horizontally over the soil's surface, so it will shade out weed seeds trying to sprout or weed seedlings trying to grow.

Short in height, so it won't get taller than crop plants and shade them out, too.

Shallow rooted, so it won't seriously compete with the crop plants for space, nutrients, and water.

---

of summer squash but basically grow the two together. The squash will quickly overtake the turnips, but it will take a while for weeds to do the same thing — especially under the dark canopy of big squash leaves.

When investigating the use of short-lived smother crops to control weeds in corn, scientists in Minnesota thought yellow mustard might do the trick. However, they found that when the corn and mustard were planted together, the mustard grew so quickly that the corn had to compete with it, and yields suffered. But if the mustard had been planted two weeks *after* the corn, the corn would have gotten the head start it needed, and the story may have had a happier ending.

The Minnesota scientists did learn that yellow mustard suppressed 66 percent of nasty weeds, which included yellow foxtail, green foxtail, lambsquarters, and redroot pigweed. If you translate this idea into a scaled-down version for a small garden, you might substitute a leafy green that you intend to eat young, such as arugula (also known as rocket), and plant it just after sunflowers or another tall crop. Instant edible smother crop!

In my spring and fall gardens, I routinely use lettuce as a smother crop, interplanting it with broccoli and always alongside peas. If left unsmothered, the open soil in the beds would be overrun with chickweed, henbit, and wild violets. With the help of lettuce (especially fast-growing leafy types), I must weed my spring garden only once or twice, and always get two crops instead of one from a limited amount of space.

In warmer weather, you might use other plants as smother crops. I often sow crowder peas in unoccupied beds in midsummer and thin back the stand (by pulling out individual plants) before sowing late crops of carrots, beets, parsley, and other vegetables that have a hard time sprouting when days are so hot that the soil heats up and dries out daily. The shade from the legumes helps keep the soil moist enough to facilitate germination. When the carrots (or whatever) attain the status of sprouts, I pull out the rest of the peas, which all the while have been fixing nitrogen and suppressing weeds.

MYSTIFY WEEDS WITH MULCHES

Almost all weed seeds need light to germinate and grow. Light is like a trigger to some weed seeds that wait in the soil for years, deactivated by darkness. Mulches control weeds by depriving them of life-giving light.

What are the best mulches for suppressing weeds? The ones you already have! In fall, spread chopped leaves over empty beds to keep chickweed and henbit at bay. If you run over the leaves with a lawn mower

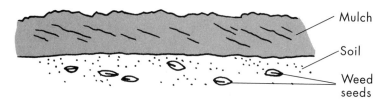

Mulch blocks the light that weed seeds need to trigger germination.

before you pile them on your soil, they will sufficiently decompose over the winter so you can simply turn them under in spring. Stockpile extra leaves to use around garden plants during the summer months.

Pine tree needles are useful, too, though they are acidic and tend to help naturally acidic soil stay that way. Use them to discourage weeds around plants that like acidic conditions, such as strawberries, azaleas, and rhododendrons.

Environmentally minded lawn-keepers are advised to let grass clippings rot where they fall, but they also make great mulch. I hook the bagger on my mower when I cut my backyard, since my family comes and goes through the back door about a hundred times a day, and loose clippings end up all through my house. The clippings go straight from the bag into flowerbeds, tucked in snugly around annual and perennial flowers. If I happen to have extra clippings, I mix them into my compost. Nothing heats up a compost heap like freshly cut grass clippings.

Slugs in the Mulch

The one disadvantage of organic mulches is that slugs and snails just love them. I went for years without serious slug problems and then accidentally imported thousands of baby slugettes in a load of rotted leaves. Two weeks of steady trapping with beer traps got the problem under control, but in some climates beer is not enough. Where slugs rule the night, try topping off a paper or cardboard mulch with sawdust, or stop mulching altogether until you get the slugs under control.

To trap slugs with beer, fill a small shallow container (like a plastic margarine tub) with beer and set it in the soil in the evening so that only the rim sticks up above the soil line. Early in the morning, go out and gather your drunken, drowned slugs. Reload the traps each night. Don't worry if you trap snails along with your slugs, for they are basically slugs with shells.

I went for years without buying mulch materials but finally decided that weathered wheat straw was worth its modest price. Unlike hay, which usually contains zillions of weed seeds, wheat and oat straw are normally pretty clean. If you can find some that's been rained on (so its value as animal food is low), buy it. Besides suppressing weeds by depriving the seeds of light, wheat and oat straw are believed to leach out chemicals that act as natural herbicides. But as long as you use them to mulch plants that are beyond the seedling stage (such as established berries or transplanted tomatoes and peppers), wheat and oat straw both have strong track records of increasing yields.

Leaves, grass clippings, straw, and other materials that rot are called organic mulches, and the material they eventually become — called humus — is nature's most fundamental soil conditioner. Yet these mulches do have a flaw when it comes to weed control. Some weeds can grow through them, a feat that becomes easier as the mulches compact, wear thin, and decompose.

You can enhance the weed-controlling ability of any organic mulch by putting sheets of newspaper or cardboard under it. Lay down newspapers two to six sheets thick directly on the ground; cut cardboard boxes to make them flat, and spread over the soil in a single layer. Top off these paper mulches with leaves, grass clippings, or straw. Newspapers also help stretch your mulch supply, since you'll need only about a 1-inch deep blanket of organic mulch instead of a 3-inch one (the usual depth required to keep weed seeds in the dark). Incidentally, don't attempt to lay down a newspaper mulch on a windy day. When a breeze picks them up, those suckers can move!

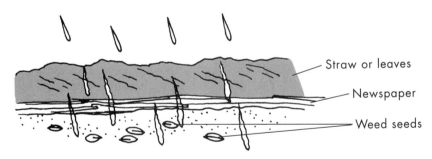

Cardboard or newspaper covered with an organic mulch makes a great weed barrier while letting rainwater filter through to the soil.

The Basics of Weed Control

Store-Bought Mulches

Roll-out mulch materials are very easy to use. Many stores offer several types, including the following:

Woven black or green polyester fabric mulch (such as the product called WeedBlock) are the most expensive kinds of roll-out mulches to buy, but they are long-lasting and work just great. Water and air pass through them, but the openings are too small for weeds. A good quality fabric mulch will last several seasons when used in shade or when protected from sunshine with an organic mulch. Gardeners who like their gardens to look extra neat and manicured love these products, and often cover them with bark nuggets or pine straw for a more natural look.

Spunbound black polyester mulches (such as Weed Barrier Mat and Weed Shield) are as easy to use as the woven types, and about as long-lasting when protected from strong sun. Tearing can occur when used in places that get heavy foot traffic. The cost is slightly less than the woven version.

Perforated black plastic is widely available at discount stores. It's basically heavy black plastic with little holes punched into it for rain to trickle through. Hot sunshine causes the plastic to degrade, so without a topping of organic mulch, the stuff is good for only one season. Relatively inexpensive, this type of mulch heats up the soil below it, so it's better in cool climates than in hot ones. A plus is that little soil moisture evaporates through the plastic, so you have to water less often.

Roll-out paper mulch (such as BioBlock) degrades over the course of a season, so you never have to pick it up — just till it under. When topped with an organic mulch, paper mulches perform beautifully, without the disposal problems of plastic. The cost is modest, too.

Board It Up

Tough perennial weeds have a habit of showing up when you're not prepared to deal with them. I keep a few short, broad boards handy and throw them on top of knots of bermudagrass to slow them down until I have a chance to dig them out. Colonies of quackgrass or johnsongrass can be held in check with boards, too, until you have time to give them the careful digging they deserve.

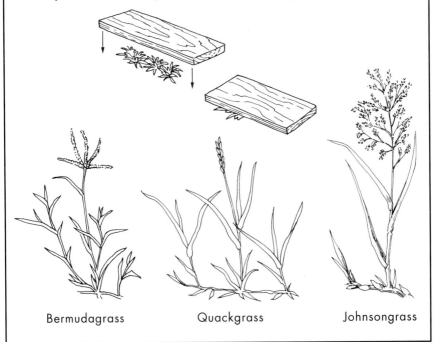

Bermudagrass   Quackgrass   Johnsongrass

Goosey Gardeners

Since the beginning of agriculture, people have tried to enlist the help of animals in controlling weeds, usually with frustrating results:

Goats are good for eating kudzu, but they'll eat other plants, too.

Chickens make great plant shredders.

Geese can be compelled to eat weeds, especially tender young grasses. However, they require as much supervision as a six-year-old, or maybe more. Never put them to work weeding a crop until you have seen for yourself that they find the weeds more palatable than the crop you're trying to get weeded.

BEWARE OF INVASIVE PLANTS

If not strictly disciplined, some plants spread so much that they become pesky weeds. You can restrain their exuberant growth in several ways, but you still have to keep a close watch on them.

Some can be kept in place by growing them in containers partially sunk into the ground, with the rim an inch or two above the soil to keep the roots from spreading. Others, like mint, are best grown between a wall (or paved area) and a space that is regularly mowed. Tall spreaders like Jerusalem artichoke and tansy are best handled by growing far from closely managed beds where they can dominate other weeds rather than cultivated plants. Here are 14 notorious spreaders and suggestions for handling them — provided you want them badly enough to put up with their invasiveness.

Crown vetch   *Coronilla varia*

An excellent ground cover for steep, eroded banks, crown vetch becomes a monster when grown in or near pampered places like gardens. It spreads via seeds and fleshy underground stems, some of which are more than 6 feet long. Avoid planting crown vetch on banks that slope toward your garden. Slopes that end at a street or ditch are more suitable sites.

Honeysuckle   *Lonicera* species

This plant's wonderfully fragrant blossoms come at a cost — runaway growth that requires a commitment to trim and prune at least twice a summer. Even well-behaved named cultivars of bush-type honeysuckles bear close watching. The trailing types demand a place of their own. If allowed to mingle with other plants, they insist on strangling their neighbors.

Jerusalem artichoke   *Helianthus tuberosus*

Grown for its nutty-tasting edible roots, this perennial sunflower dominates space with its height (to 9 feet) and by seeds and sprouting roots. Never till over a dormant cache of roots, or you'll spread them everywhere. Dig all roots from the outside of the colony yearly, in early winter, to keep the colony from getting too huge.

Morningglory   *Ipomoea hederacea*

In warm climates, the same annual morningglories that are breathtakingly beautiful on a trellis can become very pesky weeds since they twine around any other plant that's upright. Grow them far from the vegetable garden and flower garden, preferably surrounded by a large area of mowed grass.

Mints   *Mentha* **species**

The mints spread via ropy creeping underground roots, called rhizomes, which can sneak several feet — even under thick mulch or concrete. Grow them adjacent to mowed areas so you can enjoy the fragrance of the cut leaves when you mow. Or, grow them in large containers and cut back the faded flowers to keep the plants from dropping seeds. Some strains are better behaved than others.

Mugwort   *Artemisia vulgaris*

This herb is valued in fragrance gardens for its camphorlike aromatic foliage, but it's a rampant spreader that will quickly overtake other plants. Monitor new seedlings and young plantlets that pop up on the outside of the clump. Promptly pull up the ones you don't want. Cut back plants as soon as they flower to keep them from dropping seeds.

Oxeye daisy   *Chrysanthemum leucanthemum*

This lovely wild (but non-native) daisy can become a nuisance, especially in the Northwest and Midwest. But in most places, you can control oxeyes by mowing or hoeing out unwanted plants. If you like the daisies but not where they're growing, dig them in early spring and move them to your chosen spot.

Purple loosestrife   *Lythrum Salicaria*

A dramatically beautiful perennial, purple loosestrife has become such a problem in the wetlands of the upper Midwest that its cultivation there is now illegal. Until reliable sterile strains become commercially available, choose something else for your garden, like a nice monarda.

Snow-on-the-mountain   *Euphorbia marginata*

One of the largest and showiest members of the spurge family, snow-on-the-mountain spreads via seeds and has become a resented weed in parts of the Midwest. The leaves are poisonous to livestock, and the milky sap causes skin irritation, so handle with care. A much smaller Euphorbia, cypress spurge, is often grown as a ground cover and can become invasive if its spread is not controlled by the gardeners who grow it.

Tansy   *Tanacetum vulgare*

Although tansy is useful for attracting beneficial insects (and possibly repelling destructive ones), it rapidly gains dominance over other plants with its tall, robust stems, and then produces thousands of seeds. Cut it back after the flowers have hosted their mini wasp party, and promptly dig out plants that pop up where you don't want them. Better yet, grow tansy in containers so you can move it around and let different plants enjoy its beneficial aura.

Toadflax   *Linaria vulgaris*

Also known as butter-and-eggs, this delicate little wildflower sometimes gets carried away with itself, especially in northern areas where cool weather enables it to set seed very successfully. Plant it in impoverished soil where other plants refuse to grow.

Trumpet Creeper   *Campsis radicans*

When properly managed, this perennial woody vine is a fine addition to a low maintenance landscape. To limit its spread, clip off all the green seedpods you can reach before they are fully mature. Prune as needed to confine the vine to its allotted space.

Violets   *Viola papillionacea*

There are good violets and bad ones, and the common blue violet of Eastern United States is too naughty for cultivated space. Pretty flowers in early spring are no excuse for the tenacious roots of this native species or the way it reseeds so heavily that it smothers out nearby plants. Have no fear of better behaved violets, like johnny jump-ups and yellow violas, or the native birds-foot violet.

Yarrow   *Achillea millefolium; A. filipendulina*

Both species of yarrow are enthusiastic spreaders, so keep a close eye on them. Cultivated forms of both species are prettier and better behaved than the strains often sold as wildflowers, but they still need to be monitored. Pull up or dig out unwanted plants. When mowed twice a year, *A. millefolium* can make a nice ground cover.

TWELVE TIPS FOR MANAGING YOUR WEEDS

All garden situations will include weeds, no matter what. These twelve strategies can improve your garden's productivity in the presence of abundant weeds.

1. **Make your garden the right size for you.** The more space you cultivate, the more weedy visitors you can expect to appear. If you always find yourself overwhelmed by weeding chores in midsummer and at the same time grow more produce than you can use, shrink your garden to a more manageable size. The intensive gardening approach, in which every square inch of garden soil is used during every day of the growing season, also results in a reduced need to weed.

2. **Don't weed where you walk.** If you find yourself spending a lot of time weeding the pathways between garden beds or rows, stop it! You can turn those walkways into havens for beneficial insects by planting them with clovers and tufting (rather than creeping) grasses, and mowing them from time to time. Or, if your taste requires clean sweeps between rows, make your pathways naturally weed-free by lining them with bricks or stones, or mulching them heavily with a coarse organic material such as bark chunks or wood chips. Roll-type fabric weed barriers installed beneath such mulches can keep weeds out for several years.

3. **Mark your rows.** Although I, like most experienced gardeners, no longer bother with stakes, strings, and other devices that show exactly where seeds have been planted, this approach can be a great boon to beginning gardeners who are just learning to tell weed seedlings from turnips or zinnias. Later, when you have gotten to know the most common weeds in your garden, you can dispense with straight rows and begin broadcasting seeds or planting them in a nicely spaced matrix. In the vegetable garden, you might use fast-growing radishes or onions (from sets or plants) to mark rows or places in the bed where you switched from lettuce to spinach. Marigolds make good markers in annual flowerbeds.

4. **Use transplants.** Most plants do well when they begin their lives in small containers and move to the garden when they are 6 to 10 weeks old. Growing transplants enables you to pamper seedlings by giving them exactly the right amount of moisture and light, and if you grow them indoors, they benefit from warmer (or cooler) temperatures, too. All the while, they do not have to compete with weeds. If you set out seedlings when they have several leaves and are poised to grow rapidly, they will do a better job of shading out weeds, too. Plus, it's much easier to remove weeds that pop up around recognizable seedlings than to pull fast-growing weeds that tower over tiny sprouts.

5. **Seed heavily.** If you first understand that weeds are going to move in and heal over any bare spots of soil they find, it makes perfect sense to beat them to it by planting the space with lots of cultivated plants. You can then go back and thin your plants to proper spacing, which is usually more enjoyable and less tedious than weeding around a sparse stand of plants that you want to grow. Thick seeding works especially well with broad-leafed plants such as lettuce and beans. When growing small-seeded flowers (or any expensive seeds) that can't compete with weeds no matter how thickly you seed them, start them in small containers and set the plants out when they're large enough to fend for themselves.

6. **Delay planting.** If you like to push spring into gear fast and plant early, consider waiting a while with plants that won't grow well until warmer weather arrives. When warm-natured plants struggle to grow in cold soil, they are easily overtaken by weeds. And don't plant your beds all on the same day, or they'll all need weeding at the same time. Try planting different sections of your garden at two-to-three-week intervals, so that weeding and mulching can be done gradually as each set of seedlings reaches just the right size.

7. **Look for competitive varieties.** When looking at how different plants interact with weedy competitors, scientists have identified several characteristics found in plants that do especially well when forced to compete with weeds. Here are six traits of great competitors:

- *Large seeds that sprout quickly.* Beans, squash, and other large-seeded vegetables often will succeed when weeded only once or twice.
- *Large leaves.* The spreading leaves of leaf lettuce, okra, squash, sunflowers, and other plants with big leaves will deprive weed seeds and seedlings of light.
- *Numerous branches.* Plants that develop many branches and form a large, dense canopy compete well with weeds. For example, vigorous unpruned tomatoes and extra bushy beans can dominate weeds, more easily than thrifty herbs and flowers can.
- *Towering heights.* Plants that grow quite tall dominate smaller ones. Corn, pole beans, and other plants that can grow taller than the weeds will stand a better chance than plants that don't. Trellis cucumbers and peas to keep them up high.
- *Early maturing.* Fast-growing plants can produce their crops before weed competition becomes too severe.
- *High-yielding varieties.* This is probably the most important factor to consider when choosing varieties that you know you won't be able to weed regularly. If their genes make them extraordinarily vigorous and productive, weeds will be forced to take a back seat.

8. **Get them early.** If you keep weeds under control for only a month from late spring to early summer, you will have accomplished a great deal in terms of enhancing your garden's productivity. Studies with many plants, including poor competitors such as onions, beets, and carrots, have shown that the most critical period of weed control is the four weeks following germination of the seeds. After that, weeds can still interfere with the crop, but at least the cultivated plants have a fighting chance. If most of the weeds you must contend with are annuals, early control is a crucial part of the cure.

9. **Weed often.** Do it every two weeks. In a study of bell peppers conducted in California, top yields came from plots that were hand weeded every two weeks throughout the growing season. Although I've already pointed out that the critical time to keep weeds out is just after planting, bell pepper yields in plots that were kept weeded all summer were double that of plots that were weeded only twice, at two and four weeks after transplanting. The most common weeds in those plots were barnyardgrass, redroot pigweed, lambsquarters, purslane, and black nightshade, with a little velvetleaf here and there.

10. **Pull when wet, cultivate when dry.** Pay attention to the moisture content of your soil when deciding what type of weeding you will do on a given day. When the soil is wet, most weeds are easy to pull, for the water lubricates the roots and makes them slip right out. This is especially true of weeds with strong taproots, like dandelions and pigweed.

Very dry soil is great for hoeing, for almost every weed you dislodge will quickly die when it's cut off from its water supply. Hoed weeds left on the surface in dry weather promptly shrivel to death.

Soil that's neither wet nor dry is ideal for digging out weeds with spreading roots. If you plan to dig out weeds and the soil is dry, water it the day before to make your digging easier.

Nocturnal Tilling

Since exposure to light triggers germination of many weed seeds, scientists have investigated the possibility that cultivating at night might reduce weed problems. It turns out that only a few weeds can be discouraged through nocturnal tilling. Most weed seeds in the top ¼ inch of soil receive the light they need to trigger germination, regardless of when the soil is cultivated.

The Basics of Weed Control

11. Hit them when they're down.
Perennial weeds often depend on food reserves stored in underground roots or tubers. These reserves are usually lowest just before the plants flower. So, with a weed that has especially strong roots, such as field bindweed, attack it at its weakest season, when it's poised to begin flowering.

Bindweed and several other real toughies seldom perish from a single attack launched by a hoe-wielding gardener. Canada thistle, leafy spurge, horsenettle, or bindweed may show new sprouts in only a week, but wait another week or so to attack them. They won't develop new flowers in only two weeks' time, but they will use up more of the food reserves you're trying to deplete.

12. Off with their heads.
Since most of the weed seeds in your soil's weed seed bank are produced on site, preventing ripe seeds from forming is crucial to long-term weed control. Unfortunately, most weeds can grow new seed-producing parts after the first flower or seed stalk has been cut or mowed. Decapitating weeds once will do some good, but can make matters worse if you then allow several new seed-producing branches to flourish. Some weeds, such as red rooted pigweed, seem to benefit from pinching out the tops the same way that many flowers do. The pinching encourages them to develop more bushy growth, which may result in more weed seeds being produced than would have developed if the plant had been left unpinched. If you opt to mow down weeds, do it at least once a month to keep viable weed seeds from raining down.

MASQUERADING WEEDS

As you become a seasoned gardener, you will gradually become an expert at recognizing the seedlings you want to grow, as well as your weeds. This does not happen overnight, and every gardener has a story to tell about the time he thought he was growing a beautiful flower and ended up growing remarkably healthy weeds. My personal story involves Spanishneedles, which now line the back of my yard. I mistook them for yellow cosmos (the *sulphureus* species), allowed them to grow like crazy, and kept waiting for my flowers to appear. I finally got suspicious when three months passed and there were no flowers. By then, the Spanishneedles had dropped millions of seeds, and I'm fighting them to this day.

The truth is that some weeds look like cultivated plants, which is part of their self-preservation strategy. Shirley poppies look like dandelions, lambsquarters can look like radishes (at least for a while), and sorrel looks a bit like spinach. If you're new at this who's-who-of-weeds game, delay weeding until you see a pattern in the plants and weed around the row you planted. With time, recognizing the true forms of weeds and cultivated plants will become automatic.

WEEDING TOOLS

I wish I could tell you exactly which tools you will need to make your weeding easy, but different tools work better for different people. If you tend to be thrifty by nature, I suggest that you begin your quest for the perfect weeding tools at a local hardware or discount store. There you will encounter a nice assortment of affordable tools.

As your beginning armaments for your war on weeds, choose a hoe and a spade with handles long enough for your height (taller people need longer handles). Also get a long-handled pronged hoe (also called a cultivator) and a digging fork. The handles on these tools are often short compared to those on hoes, but you must bend over and put your shoulders behind them to make them work well, anyway.

Heat Treatment for Weeds

Perhaps you've heard the news that some farmers are using special flame-throwing devices to control weeds, and some parks have invested in weeding machines that use steam to boil weeds to death. Both stories are true, but don't get excited about applying these methods to your garden. Although you can buy weed flamers, they are not for every gardener or every weed. Woody weeds often survive flaming, and since the heat kills only the top parts of the weeds, weeds that can regrow from their roots often do exactly that. If you live in a dry climate, weed flaming may even be illegal.

As for the steam method, you can use good old boiling water to get rid of weeds growing in the cracks of a driveway or sidewalk, but you might kill more plants than you intend to if you start pouring boiling water into your garden. And then there's the possibility that you might stumble and fall while carrying a pot of boiling water. Hmm . . . a hoe is starting to sound good, isn't it?

Now, about hoes. There are a dozen different kinds, and I think the lightweight ones are easiest to use. The tool most people picture in their minds when they think of "hoe" is the American hoe, which works quite well when the blade is regularly sharpened. However, I like what's called a gooseneck hoe better, mostly because the blade is smaller and lighter, and the long curved neck makes it easier to manipulate in close spaces.

A couple of years ago I bought a tool called a swoe, which has a small pseudo-rectangular blade with a pointed tip at one end attached to a long handle at the other end. I have found it wonderfully useful for my garden's worst weeds, bermudagrass, and wild violets, which I can dig out with the swoe without bending over.

If the people at your favorite hardware store look confused when you ask for a gooseneck hoe or a swoe, don't be surprised, for there is no standardization at all in what various hand tools are called. This is another advantage of shopping retail — you can actually pick up and feel the tools before you buy them.

Among short-handled hand tools, I have found no tools that do a better job than my own fingers (for pulling), a slender knife (for cutting), and an old kitchen fork (for loosening). There is a hand tool that goes by the names fishtail weeder, V-weeder, dandelion weeder, and asparagus knife that is very helpful for prying up weeds with tenacious roots, such as dandelion or pigweed. A similar tool called a Cape Cod weeder is useful for prying up weeds with fibrous roots, such as plantain.

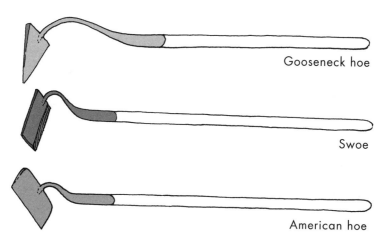

Gooseneck hoe

Swoe

American hoe

Regardless of the hoe you choose, make sure the length of the handle is compatible with your height.

The Basics of Weed Control

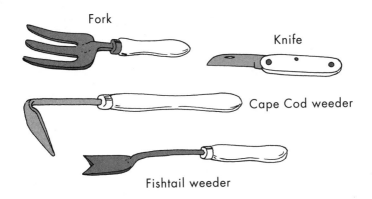

Fork

Knife

Cape Cod weeder

Fishtail weeder

Hand weeding is most effective when a few simple short-handled tools are used.

Just as different people have strong preferences for certain tools, different weeds require different tools, too. As you get to know your predominant weeds and how they grow, you will have a much better idea about the tools that will be best for you. Talk to other gardeners in your area about the tools that work best for them and try them out yourself. Then, when you settle on certain tools that you really like, invest in the best versions you can find — really well-made tools that will stand the test of time.

Keep an open mind where weeding tools are concerned. Hardly a year goes by that some enterprising gardener does not come up with a new weeding tool that purports to solve all your weeding problems with a flick of the wrist. A corner of my garage is a monument to such experiments. Some work and some don't, at least for me.

Make It Easy on Your Knees

Hoeing can be done standing up, but most hand weeding requires you to squat, kneel, or sit while you get the job done. My preference is to sit, and I do it on a dense foam pad that I've had for years. A neighbor uses an old stadium seat, and the garden catalogs sell kneeling pads made especially for this purpose. All weeders need one of these or something equally effective, both to keep their clothes clean and to make weeding easier.

The Basics of Weed Control

About Herbicides

Herbicides are chemicals that kill plants. Conventional farmers rely on them heavily, but I think gardeners are better off using them only for emergencies. It's a purity issue, for all chemical herbicides are highly toxic and definitely do not fit into the descriptive category of "earth safe." In this book, the only time I have suggested a chemical herbicide is for poison ivy. Since poison ivy is not "people safe," I think there's a rational balance there.

You will not find me recommending so-called natural herbicides, either, for I have been disappointed with how well they work. Spray-on organic herbicides are basically soap sprays, and they do manage to kill the top parts of young seedling weeds. However, they are useless against older plants, and even young treated weeds often manage to grow back from their uninjured roots. Considering the time involved in mixing and applying these products, their short-term benefits, and the ever-present risk of injuring non-weeds, I think they're a poor substitute for more traditional methods of weed control such as hands-on weeding.

Old-time methods of chemical control involving salt and vinegar aren't safe, either, for they destroy many soil-dwelling microcritters and may make the soil unfit for plants. For weeds, there are no environmentally safe miracle cures that come in bottles.

Weed Disposal

What are you to do with your weeds once you get them out of the garden? Young weeds often can be laid on the surface of the soil where they will dry into mulch, or you can chop them into your compost heap when they are succulent and green. But watch out if the weeds are already in flower, even if you don't think they are carrying mature seeds. Some weeds, like chickweed and purslane, can continue to develop seeds after you pull the plants from the soil.

Some of the toughest weeds have a miraculous talent for surviving the heat and stress of the hottest compost heap. However, these same weeds may be dried to death and then composted after they are thoroughly dead. Scientists have found that roots and rhizomes of some of the real toughies — nutsedge, bermudagrass, quackgrass, and Canada thistle — lose viability when air dried until their water content drops below 20 percent. Although I cannot tell you how to judge when discarded weeds have reached that 20 percent moisture level, I can report on the drying method that works for me.

First, on the day that I pull out these troublesome weeds, I pile them loosely in a black plastic wheelbarrow and park it in the sun for a day or two. If rain is expected, I move the wheelbarrow to a dry place (such as my garage) so the weeds won't get wet. I often leave the weeds in the wheelbarrow until I need it for something else. Then, I dump the weeds in a pile that cooks in the sun and never gets watered. In rainy weather, you can stuff the weeds into a black plastic bag.

I make sure the plant parts are thoroughly dead by spreading them out, wetting them down, and seeing if there are any signs of life. Only then will I chop and mix the nastiest of the nasty weeds into my compost heap.

THE BRIGHTER SIDE OF WEEDS

Since gardening always involves opening up the soil and leaving it exposed to the natural elements from time to time, all gardens will host weeds. Hand weeding can be an enjoyable activity and can help your garden in other ways, since it places you on eye level with your plants, where you may notice other problems, such as insects or diseases, that require prompt attention.

Weeding is good exercise, too. A recent survey of exertion values of various physical activities ranked weeding alongside moderate bicycling and water aerobics. When digging out tough perennial weeds, you use as much energy as you would in a low-impact aerobics workout!

And finally, there are fewer experiences that leave you with the satisfied feeling you get when looking at a lovely bed of spinach, or flowerbed on the brink of bloom, that you've just cleaned of every last weed.

CHAPTER 3

A GALLERY
OF
MAINSTREAM WEEDS

YOU WILL FIND most of the weeds in your garden listed in this chapter, including all weeds that grow as bushes, upright plants, and low-spreading mats. Weeds that are grasslike in appearance follow in Chapter 4, and those that run about as vines are described in Chapter 5.

Weeds often go by many different names, most of which are listed within each entry. The most common alternate names for the weeds are listed first; the most obscure, last. If you cannot find a weed that you know only by its nickname, check the index before you give up. Also keep your mind open to the possibility that a weed that is not supposed to grow in your area may be in your garden anyway. As discussed in Chapter 1, weed seeds have ingenious ways of traveling from place to place.

Whenever a weed is closely related to a cultivated plant, I have made a note of it and tried to identify the most garden-worthy cultivars by their botanical names. Frequently, if a weedy species likes your garden, its cultivated cousin will have what it takes to grow successfully as well.

The weeds are listed in alphabetical order by their most commonly used name. Chapter 6, Weedy Family Relations, sorts these garden weeds into their botanical families.

Black medic

Medicago lupulina

Black clover, yellow trefoil, none-such, hop medic, hop clover

Site, soil, and season: Basically a beneficial weed, black medic occurs most often in poor, dry soils in full sun. Plants begin blooming in midspring and continue blooming sporadically all summer.

Description: Black medic is a beneficial weed that takes its job of improving poor soil very seriously. One look and you can tell it's a clover, and you may have called it yellow clover. However, the stems of black medic are almost woody compared to other clovers, and its small yellow flower clusters are one fourth the size of those produced by white Dutch clover. Underground, black medic grows on a thin root system, too. However, those roots fix nitrogen and leave behind beneficial bacteria that can help other members of the pea family feed themselves.

To identify this weed, look for leaves comprising 3 leaflets, each with a fold down the center. There is a small raised bump where each leaf joins the stem. The stems branch and spread 1 to 2 feet from the base. Small yellow flower clusters emerge on short stalks all along the stems at leaf joints and at the ends of the branches. When the tiny seeds are mature, they are each enclosed in a hard black pod.

Control: If your garden soil is reasonably fertile, you will rarely see this weed growing there — only occasional upstarts from seeds dropped by birds. The appearance of numerous plants suggests that your soil is not yet ready for gardening and needs improvement, or that it has been used as pasture. Years ago black medic was used for pasture forage and cover cropping, but it has since been replaced with vetches, clovers, and other medics that are even better at fixing nitrogen.

Individual black medic plants are easily pulled out, or you can allow them to grow for a while and then mow over them before they develop seeds. Allow black medic to grow if you have no immediate plans for the spot it occupies, for it will do more good than harm. ∎

Black medic

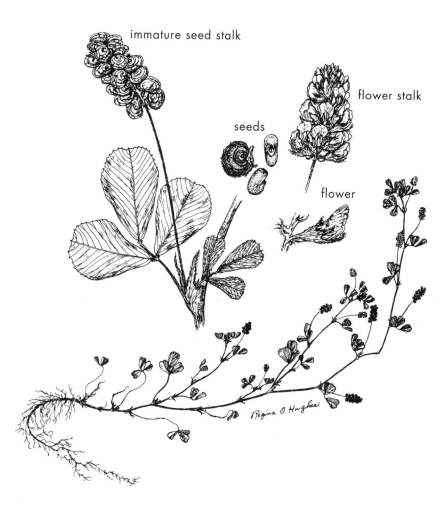

immature seed stalk

flower stalk

seeds

flower

Regina O. Hughes

Black medic

Life cycle: Annual, winter annual, or short-lived perennial
Origin: Eurasia
Range: Throughout the United States and southern Canada

Flower color: Yellow
Height: 1–2 feet (30–61 cm)

Black medic

Tall buttercup

Ranunculus acris

Crowfoot, butter flower, blister plant, butter rose

Creeping buttercup

Ranunculus repens

Crowfoot, butter flower, blister plant, butter rose

Site, soil, and season: The buttercups like damp soils in gardens, pastures, or lawns. Grazing animals rarely eat buttercups since the leaves and stems contain an acrid sap that can irritate the animals' mouths. This gives the plants a wonderful opportunity to grow, and then birds pick up the seeds and spread them around. Tall buttercup, a common pasture weed, often spreads into gardens this way. Creeping buttercup is very common in moist, cool climates such as the Pacific Northwest and New England. Buttercups like full sun or partial shade. Bloom time is late spring in mild winter climates and late summer where winters are so cold that the plants remain dormant until April or May.

Description: Young buttercup plants look so refined that they might pass for ground-hugging celery, at least for a while. The roundish leaves with wavy edges found on young plants resemble flat parsley, only broader and lighter green in color. Leaves of creeping buttercup are somewhat hairy, but young leaves of tall buttercup are glossy.

After passing winter and early spring as small rosettes, buttercups burst into flower in mid-to-late spring. Quite suddenly a central stem elongates and flowers, followed by other branches that arise from the plant's central crown or branch out from the plant's main stem. The rich yellow color of this weed's flower almost qualifies it as an ornamental, and in fact the blossoms blend well with those of more refined flowers. After the petals fall, circular seed heads composed of numerous fat green seed capsules slowly ripen on the plants.

Creeping buttercup is an aggressive spreader. Low stems spread from the main crown and become tufted with little plantlets, the same way strawberry runners give rise to new plants. Creeping buttercups often develop roots before the plantlets even touch the soil.

Control: With the annual buttercups, pull out the plants whenever you like, but before mature seeds develop. The plants are easiest to pull after they have elongated in preparation for flowering. Young plants grow so close to the ground that they are best removed with a sharp hoe.

If you like buttercup flowers, you can let the plants stay in the garden until after the first flowers appear. Dispose of the plants in a dry heap and compost them after they are thoroughly dead.

To get rid of creeping buttercup, dig out the plants from beneath when the soil is moderately damp. Lift the entire plants with roots attached, for new plants can form from root pieces left behind in the soil. Digging out creeping buttercup from a lawn will leave a bare space, so be prepared to fill it immediately with sod or grass seed that matches the rest of your lawn. Go back in the fall and pull out any small plants that may have emerged in the site. ■

fruiting head

seed

Creeping buttercup

Life cycle: Perennial; often a winter
  annual where summers are hot
Origin: Europe
Range: Wild species of *Ranunculus* grow
  throughout North America

Flower color: Yellow
Height: 8–18 inches (20–46 cm)

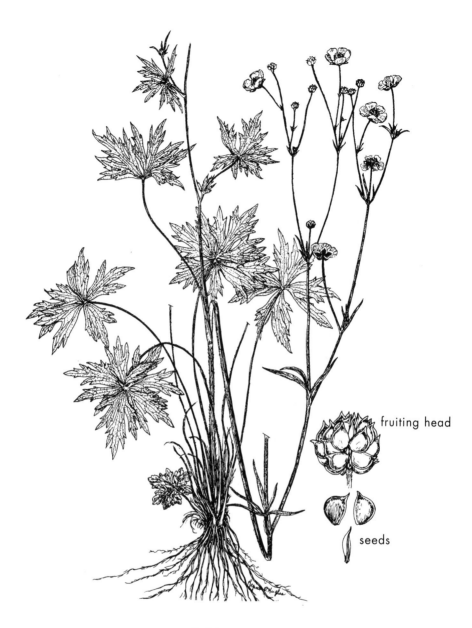

fruiting head

seeds

Tall buttercup

Life cycle: Perennial; often winter annual
where summers are hot

Origin: Europe

Range: Wild species of *Ranunculus* grow
throughout North America

Flower color: Yellow

Height: 1–3 feet (30–91 cm)

Virginia buttonweed	*Diodia virginiana*
Poorjoe	*Diodia teres*

Buttonweed

Site, soil, and season: Virginia buttonweed usually stays green all year, though it does not grow much during the winter months. It grows well in good garden soil and is also very adept at colonizing lawns. Poorjoe sprouts in late spring, when the soil is warm, and flowers in midsummer. It often grows in dry, unimproved soil that is slightly acidic.

Description: Virginia buttonweed is a low, mat-forming plant with dark green leaves and tiny white star-shaped flowers with 4 petals that form right along the stems. Narrow leaves about 1 inch long grow opposite each other from the stems. The stems, leaves, and seedpods are covered with downy hairs. In cool weather the stems may be reddish in color, but they become green in summer.

Small rosettes of green growth often stand through winter and grow continuously all summer. An individual plant growing in good soil can form a ground cover 2 square feet in size. Small fibrous roots develop wherever stems lie on the soil. When mowed, the plants lie very close to the ground and are easy to see after the surrounding grass is mowed.

After the white flowers fade, Virginia buttonweed develops fat green egg-shaped seedpods with a tiny set of green wings on the tops. The pods dry into leathery coverings for the brown seeds.

Poorjoe is like a lightweight version of its perennial cousin, only its flowers are pink or white and much smaller than those of Virginia buttonweed. The leaves are slightly smaller and less hairy, and the plants tend to grow semi-upright. They usually begin to flower when 6 to 8 inches tall. The seed capsule "buttons" have 3 or 4 leafy wings at the top. In mature poorjoe plants, the lowest stems appear brown, and those near branching joints often show a reddish tint. Stems are light green near the tips.

Control: Virginia buttonweed can be pulled up, but the stems often break off, leaving viable roots in the soil. In gardens, try to dig out the plants. In the lawn, either welcome Virginia buttonweed or pull out the stems by hand every three weeks until it disappears. Mowing seems to encourage this plant.

Poorjoe's roots are skimpy, so it's easy to pull out at any stage of growth. ■

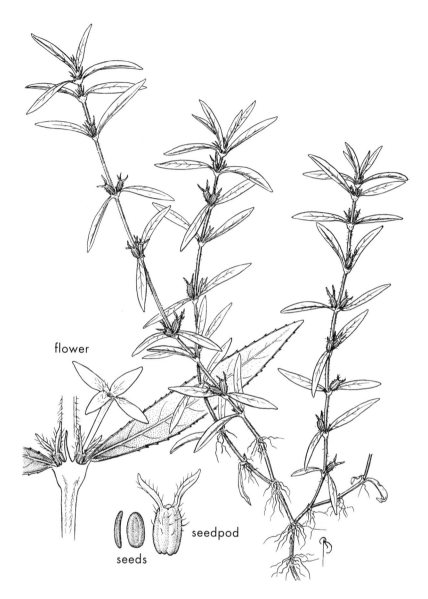

flower

seeds

seedpod

Virginia buttonweed

Life cycle: Perennial
Origin: Eastern United States
Range: From Connecticut westward to central Kansas, and southward to the Gulf of Mexico

Flower color: White
Height: 6–8 inches (15–20 cm)

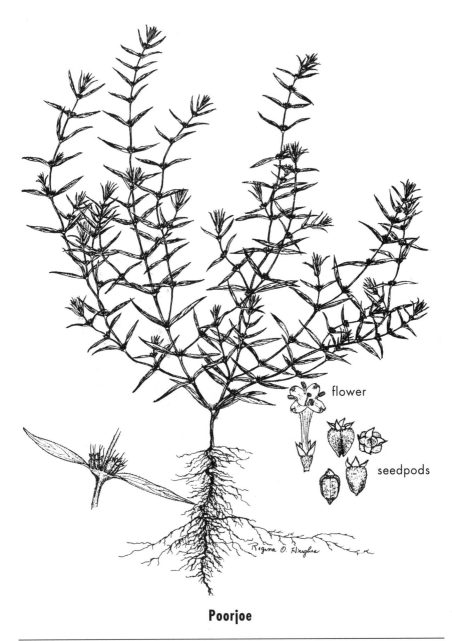

flower

seedpods

Poorjoe

Life cycle: Summer annual
Origin: Eastern United States
Range: From Connecticut westward to
   Central Kansas, and southward to the
   Gulf of Mexico

Flower color: Pink or white
Height: 8–18 inches (20–46 cm)

Canada thistle
Cirsium arvense

Creeping thistle, small-flowered thistle, perennial thistle, green thistle

Site, soil, and season: Canada thistle grows best in heavy, moist soils, but easily becomes established in diverse environments when seeds from meadows and roadside plants blow about with the wind. Seedlings and young plants appear in early spring and produce flowers from midsummer until frost. Plants in the far north produce more seeds than those in the southern range. It is a persistent and common weed northward from a horizontal line between Virginia and Central California. It is considered noxious.

Description: Young Canada thistle plants arise from the soil on a single stem and appear first as a rosette of spiny leaves. The leaves are variable in shape. They often have numerous pointed lobes but sometimes do not. They almost always have crinkled edges and spines. The spines can scratch you but are not stiff enough to actually puncture skin.

As the stem grows longer, the new leaves grow alternately rather than opposite one another, and mature leaves often become hairy on the undersides. By the time a seedling plant is a foot tall, it will have developed a stout fleshy taproot. Most Canada thistle plants grow from horizontal roots that spread from the taproot and persist in the soil from year to year. If you dig up a thistle plant and find that it grows from a bud attached to a stringy horizontal root, your prize is probably a Canada thistle.

When Canada thistle flowers, the plants branch at the top and the blossoms appear as hairy tufts ½ to ¾ inches wide. They are usually rosy purple but are occasionally lavender or white.

The first flowers that appear may develop mature seeds by the time the plants finish flowering. Seeds are ⅛ inch long, oblong and often curved, with downy white hairs attached to one end. By summer's end, a parent plant is usually surrounded by a small army of plantlets that have grown from its wandering roots.

Control: Several minor thistles resemble Canada thistle, and none of them should be allowed to grow in or near a garden. At the very least, lop off their heads as soon as the flowers appear, if not before. Unfortunately, with Canada thistle simple decapitation is not nearly enough.

To eradicate a dense stand of Canada thistle, begin by allowing the plants to grow up in spring. Then, when they are quite robust and large (but not yet flowering), mow them down. The objective is to make them use up some of the food they have accumulated in their roots. Allow a second flush of growth and mow again.

With the foundation roots of the colony weakened, turn up the soil and allow it to bake in the summer sun. If you use a rototiller, stop and clean the tines before using the machine in soil that is not infested with this weed. Even small bits of root can sprout into new plants.

Following a rain, you still may see new thistle plants sprouting up here and there. If the space is small and you have long-term plans for it that will make it impossible to work (like planting a mixed perennial border), go ahead and dig in manure or other soil conditioners and cover the space with clear or black plastic for a few weeks. Then sow a quick cover crop of bush beans, peas, or other nitrogen-fixing green manure. After the cover crop is killed by cold weather, dig out any small thistle plants that may have emerged.

Small infestations can be carefully dug out. Since you're really after the roots, begin working from the outside of the clump, and loosen the soil with a digging fork. By the time you reach the area beneath the plant, you should be able to lift a sizable mass of roots without having them break off into pieces.

Once Canada thistle has infested a spot, there is always a possibility that it will return, since some root pieces are several feet deep, beyond the reach of your shovel. Yet the constant cultivating and mulching that goes on in closely managed vegetable gardens frustrates this weed's enthusiasm so well that after a few seasons, no further cure is needed. ■

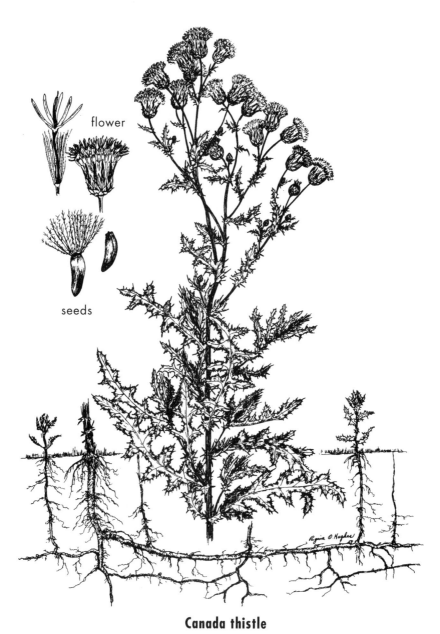

flower

seeds

Canada thistle

Life cycle: Perennial
Origin: Europe
Range: Throughout the northern half of the continent

Flower color: Rosy purple, occasionally lavender or white
Height: 2–5 feet (61–152 cm)

Canada thistle

Carolina geranium
Geranium carolinianum

Wild geranium, cranesbill

Site, soil, and season: This weed usually grows as a winter annual from Zone 6 southward, while in northern areas it is a springtime weed. It is adapted to many types of soil and can tolerate acidic conditions. Carolina geranium is seen in both sun and shade, and is as at home along dry roadsides as it is in moist gardens.

Description: Carolina geranium seems quite harmless when it is young but becomes unsightly in flowerbeds when it suddenly reaches full size in late spring. The young plants are small, circular rosettes with only a few stems emerging from the central crown. Single leaves borne at the ends of the soft purplish stems are roughly circular in outline and divided into 5 (sometimes 3) deeply cut divisions, like fringed fingers on a hand. Leaves are darker on the top than underneath. Leaf veins are clearly raised on leaf undersides. The stems and leaves are covered with short, downy hairs.

Following a few warm spring days, the plants suddenly double in size and develop new branches attached to the main stems at knobby rounded elbows. Small clusters of pale purple 5-petaled flowers then open beneath the shelter of the topmost leaves. A few weeks later, these flower clusters develop into masses of round black seeds.

Control: Most weeds are more troublesome to farmers than they are to gardeners, but this one specializes in colonizing flowerbeds and gardens that are cultivated in fall. Pull the seedlings when they are young. If you can't grab the small rosettes well, pull them up by slipping a fork beneath the central crown and prying them from the soil. If you wait too long, older plants tend to break off when you pull them. Hoe older plants by cutting them off just below the soil's surface. Plants that do not hold mature seeds may be composted. ∎

Wildflower or Weed?

Carolina geranium has a taprooted perennial cousin, also called cranesbill *(Geranium maculatum)*, that's better known as a wildflower than a weed. It has much larger leaves than weedy cranesbill. If perennial cranesbill is growing where you don't want it, dig to expose its roots, and it will quickly perish.

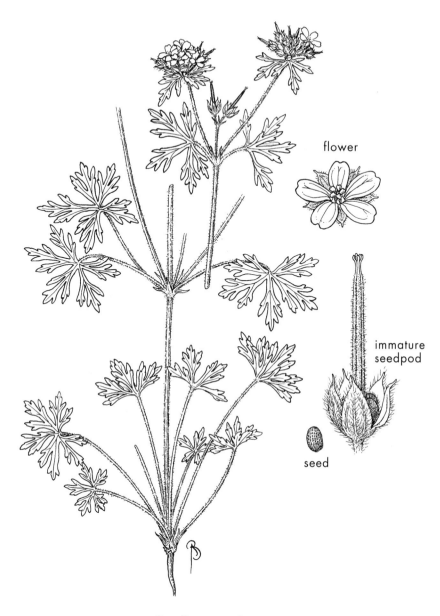

flower

immature
seedpod

seed

Carolina geranium

Life cycle: Summer annual or winter annual
Origin: Eastern United States
Range: Throughout North America

Flower color: Pale purple
Height: 6–16 inches (15–40.5 cm)

Carpetweed

Mollugo verticillata

Indian chickweed, whorled chickweed, devil's grip

Site, soil, and season: This is a garden weed that seldom shows until the soil is warm. Its specialty is forming a green rug over loose, open soil. Sandy spots are a favorite home.

Description: If all weeds were as well behaved as this one, gardeners would never need hoes. The tiny seedlings appear in late spring as small rosettes that can fit on a dime. The smooth, oblong leaves are green with pinkish stems toward the center of the crown. When the ground-hugging plant has 6 to 8 leaves, stems begin to grow outward, hugging the ground, and small tufts of leaves develop at 1-inch intervals down the stems. The stems do not develop supplemental roots though they lie right on the ground. In a few short weeks, the plant becomes a green carpet. When multiple plants grow close together, they form a living ground cover.

Tiny white flowers with 5 petals grow on slender stems from each knot of leaves. Little orange kidney-shaped seeds develop inside green capsules after the flowers fade.

Control: Some gardeners allow this weed to grow since it helps smother out other weeds and stays so close to the ground that it does not block light from cultivated plants. But if you don't want carpetweed, simply hoe it down and cover the soil where it wants to grow with any type of mulch. Individual plants can be pulled up when the soil is wet by firmly grasping the central crown. ∎

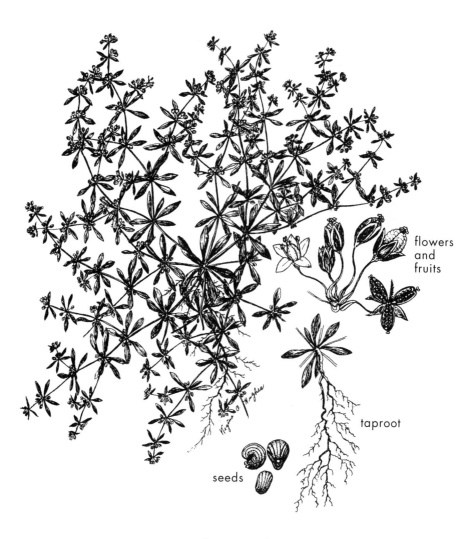

flowers
and
fruits

taproot

seeds

Carpetweed

Life cycle: Summer annual
Origin: Africa and tropical America
Range: Throughout most of temperate
North America, especially the
eastern half

Flower color: White
Height: 4 inches (10 cm)

Chickweed

Stellaria media

Starweed, starwort, winter-weed, satin flower, tongue grass, chick wittles, passerina, clucken wort, skirt button, stitchwort

Site, soil, and season: Chickweed generally grows as a winter annual, sprouting from fall to early spring and setting seeds while the weather remains quite cold. In mild winter climates, chickweed blooms and sets seeds sporadically all winter, whenever the weather briefly turns warm. The plants are tremendously cold hardy. Chickweed grows best in moist, fertile soil with a near neutral pH. It can grow successfully in sun or partial shade. It is very common in vegetable gardens, flowerbeds, and new lawns.

Description: Chickweed is a very small plant at first, but quickly grows into a lush green mat that covers the ground. The small, ½-inch-long oval-shaped leaves are pointed at the end and appear opposite one another on the stems. The stems may begin showing flowers when only 4 inches long but usually reach at least a foot in length. The stems hug the ground as a tangled mat in cold weather and reach upward in warmer weather or when shaded by taller plants.

Small white flowers open fully only when it's sunny, but they partially open on warm, cloudy days. Some seeds are mature by the time a plant is finished flowering, and seeds continue to mature after a plant is pulled up. A single chickweed plant can produce 2,500 to 15,000 seeds. Since chickweed thrives in rich, organically improved soil, many gardeners find that improving their soil leads to lush winter crops of chickweed.

Fortunately, chickweed is edible, which should be a relief to gardeners who have been picking it out of their lettuce and spinach lest it be a dangerous addition to salads. The flavor of chickweed is an earthy version of spinach, whether raw or cooked.

Control: How you control chickweed depends on where it is growing. When thick mats cover your resting vegetable beds early in the winter, you might turn the plants under and put them to work as a green manure. Do this only during the first half of winter. By February, the plants will be more likely to come back to life than rot when turned under.

In early spring, use a pronged hoe to comb through thick stands of chickweed. When the stems become knotted around the tines of the tool, twist it in a circle, so that the twist of the hoe head pries the plants

flower

capsule

seeds

Common chickweed

Life cycle: Winter annual

Origin: Europe

Range: Throughout North America

Flower color: White

Height: 6–12 inches (15–40.5 cm)

Chickweed

Eek! A Mouse!

If your weed looks a lot like chickweed, but the leaves are dark green and hairy instead of light green and shiny, you're probably looking at mouse-ear chickweed, *Cerastium vulgatum*. This hardy perennial weed often grows as a winter annual, and its tiny white flowers appear a few weeks later in spring than those of common chickweed. Don't be surprised to find the two chickweeds growing together among your strawberries or snuggled close to the buds of sleeping peonies. Control mouse-ear chickweed exactly like common chickweed.

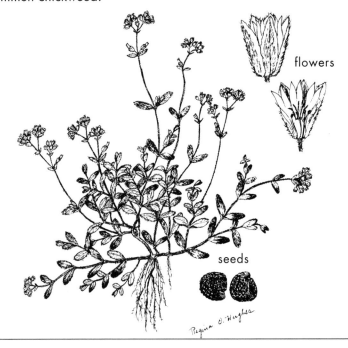

flowers

seeds

from the soil. Remove chunks of chickweed from the tines and dump them in a waste place.

To remove individual chickweed plants that have nestled close to the crowns of hardy flowers, use an ordinary kitchen fork (for big jobs, use a serving fork). Slip the tines of the fork under the primary crown of the plant, just at the soil line or slightly beneath it. Twist the fork as you would to wind up spaghetti and pull the weed away at a 45-degree angle. This method takes up very little soil, and you can get very close to your flowers without injuring them.

Chickweed in lawns is a cosmetic problem, especially when the plants turn yellow and die back in late spring or early summer. One method that's been used for 50 years is to locate the central crown of the offending chickweed plants, step on it and twist with the toe of your shoe, and then place a small cone of high nitrogen granular fertilizer on it. Or simply pull out the plant when the soil is wet and sprinkle the ground with grass seed that matches the rest of your lawn.

If you have harvested a number of chickweed plants that have developed mature seeds, don't compost them. Chickweed seeds can germinate after being buried for 10 years and easily survive the digestive tracts of horses, cows, pigs, and sheep. When using chickweed as a cover crop that will be turned under, mow the mats regularly to keep flowers and seeds from developing and then cultivate the soil in very early spring, as soon as it is dry enough to work. ■

Oldfield cinquefoil

Potentilla simplex

Common cinquefoil, barren strawberry, five fingers

Rough cinquefoil

Potentilla norvegica

Tall five fingers

Site, soil, and season: Rough cinquefoil spreads by seeds, which often sprout in both fall and spring. The plants flower in mid-to-late spring. This weed grows best in full sun or partial shade. Oldfield cinquefoil is much smaller and grows as a ground cover in partially shaded places or in small colonies in the lawn. In gardens, both cinquefoils usually occur in ornamental beds that are seldom cultivated.

Description: A huge size difference separates these two species. In flower, oldfield cinquefoil resembles yellow-flowered strawberries, only with leaves divided into 5 "fingers" with saw-toothed edges. The plants produce short runners in typical strawberry style; older plants show woody crowns like those found on strawberries, too.

Rough cinquefoil is well suited to life as a garden weed, since it spreads by seeds, which sprout in fall as well as in the spring. If the ground remains uncultivated until midspring, the plants suddenly grow upright stems topped by small yellow flowers. Individual leaves (divided into only 3 fingers) with serrated edges develop alternately (rather than opposite each other) from the stem. Inside each tiny flower, you can usually see more than a dozen long pistils. Bees often visit the pollen-rich flowers.

Control: You may decide to accept a small colony of oldfield cinquefoil in your lawn, for the yellow flowers are pretty and the plants are not aggressive spreaders when they are regularly mowed. If a colony gets out of control in a perennial bed, pull up the plants when the soil is wet.

Rough cinquefoil is easily killed by hoeing or cultivating the soil. Individual plants may be pulled up, but be sure to get the plant base when you pull. If it is left behind, a new stem will likely sprout up to replace the one you removed.

Cultivated counterparts: Several potentillas have been selected and bred into wonderful ornamental plants. If weedy cinquefoils are turning up in your garden, take that as a hint from nature that the cultivated forms are well suited to your site. Two species often used as ground covers are *Potentilla tridentata* and *P. neumanniana*. Upright shrubby cinquefoils are usually cultivars of *P. fruticosa.* There is even a fine herbaceous perennial cinquefoil, *P. atrosanguinea* (Gibson's scarlet), which bears dazzling red flowers. ■

seeds

flower and calyx

Oldfield cinquefoil

Life cycle: Perennial	**Flower color:** Yellow
Origin: Eastern United States	**Height:** 6 inches (15 cm)
Range: Eastern United States	

calyx and flower

seeds

Rough cinquefoil

Life cycle: Winter annual

Origin: Eurasia and native

Range: Throughout much of North
America

Flower color: Yellow

Height: 2–3 feet (61–91 cm)

Cocklebur

Xanthium pennsylvanicum,
Xanthium strumarium

Clotbur, sheepbur, button bur, ditch bur

Site, soil, and season: Cocklebur seeds begin sprouting in spring, and more seedlings appear later in summer following rains. Primarily a weed of sunny fields, cocklebur needs at least a half day of sun. It adapts to many types of soils and often hides beneath corn until the corn plants begin to dry, at which time the cocklebur plants explode with new growth and fill the vacant space.

Description: Cocklebur seedlings have large, medium green leaves that are lighter green on the undersides than on the tops. The first leaves have smooth edges, and the seedling stem usually has a reddish base. Later leaves have toothed edges, are roughly triangular in shape, and 3 to 5 inches across. Leaves emerge alternately (rather than opposite one another) from the main stem.

By the time a cocklebur plant has 6 leaves, you will see a heavy sprinkling of reddish brown specks all over the main stem. New leaves emerging from the plant's center will have a dusty, frosty appearance.

They may flower and set seed only 55 days or so after they sprout, or it can take twice that long. The flowers hardly look like flowers at all since their petals are so small; they grow on little stems that emerge from places where the leaves join the main stem.

The flower stage passes quickly as the plants get on with the business of making burs. Immature burs are green, and mature ones dry to woody brown. The burs are about ½ inch long, covered with hooked barbs, usually with 2 extra-long barbs at one end. Inside, each bur carries 2 seeds. One seed germinates the following year, and the other waits an additional year (or more) to sprout. A large cocklebur plant can produce 400 seeds in a season.

Cocklebur plants shade other crops and can host powdery mildew. The young seedlings are poisonous to livestock. Dogs, people, and other animals spread the seeds when the burs become tangled in fur, socks, and pants legs.

Control: Young plants are easy to pull up or hoe down. They can be laid on the ground beneath other plants to dry into mulch, or you can chop them into the compost heap. Older plants develop woody taproots that make them hard to pull. Cut them down below the soil line with a sharp spade. Topping the plants usually results in new stems emerging from the stubs left behind.

If you face a large population of plants holding green burs, cut them down with a swingblade or weed trimmer with blade attachment. Gather together plants that have mature brown burs and dump them in deep shade to rot. Never turn under viable seeds, for they can survive in your soil's seed bank for many years. ■

Temporarily Toxic

Cocklebur seeds and young seedlings are poisonous to humans and livestock, but the toxicity of the plants quickly decreases after the first true leaves appear. The seedlings slightly resemble those of jimsonweed (page 84), which are poisonous, too.

The juice of the cocklebur plant is yellow, and was used as a hair tint by blondes of ancient Greece.

seedling

bur

seed

Common cocklebur

Life cycle: Summer annual
Origin: Mississippi Valley, Eurasia, and
    Central America
Range: Throughout most of North
America, predominantly in places
    where corn is grown
Flower color: Green
Height: 1–4 feet (30–122 cm)

Cocklebur

Creeping bellflower

Campanula rapunculoides

Bellflower, creeping harebell, bluebells of Scotland

Site, soil, and season: Creeping bellflower dies back to its roots in winter, and new growth appears in early spring. New seedlings may appear in spring or fall. It is most often seen along roadsides and in waste places but can also be a problem in lawns and flower gardens.

Description: Bellflower is easy to identify by its pretty bell-shaped purple flowers or by its not-so-pretty tuberous roots. The nodding flowers are 1 inch long and grow from a flowering spike. The lowest flowers open first, the top ones last.

Young seedlings have heart-shaped leaves that grow from a central crown. In late spring the plants send up a single erect stem studded with elongated heart-shaped leaves which grow alternately (rather than opposite each other) along the stem. The flower spikes appear when the stems are 1 to 3 feet tall. When broken, the stems bleed a milky juice.

Below ground, short runners grow from the main roots, and tubers that look like skinny sweet potatoes develop along these runners. Frequently they are forked into two joined pieces. When bellflower is left to grow freely, plants form dense patches, and many tuberous roots can be found about 6 inches below the soil's surface.

Control: Dig out the plants, taking up as much of the roots as you can. Harvest the flowers (they make nice cut flowers) rather than letting them develop mature seeds. Despite its good looks, creeping bellflower is too aggressive to coexist with other perennial flowers and should be relegated to wild sites where its exuberant growth will not interfere with other plants.

Cultivated Counterparts: If every family has its black sheep, bellflower is the black sheep of the Campanula family. Many Campanula cousins include bellflower in their common names, including *C. glomerata* (clustered bellflower) and *C. persicifolia* (willow bellflower). These and many other well-behaved campanulas can be planted in perennial beds and borders without worry. ■

Creeping bellflower

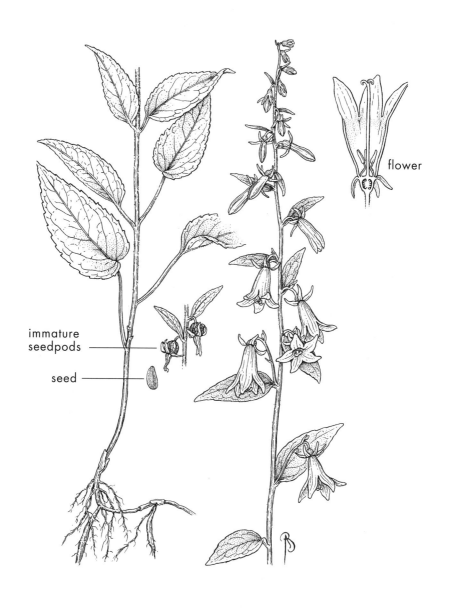

immature
seedpods

seed

flower

Creeping bellflower

Life cycle: Perennial

Origin: Eurasia; brought to North
    America as a flower garden plant

Range: Newfoundland to Missouri,

westward to Colorado

Flower color: Purple

Height: 2–4 feet (61–122 cm)

Creeping bellflower

Dandelion   *Taraxacum officinale*

Lion's-tooth, blowball, cankerwort

Site, soil, and season: Dandelions grow in all types of soil, in sun or shade, on dry slopes or damp low land. You will find them in lawns, perennial beds, and gardens.

Description: The first wildflower that shows its colors in spring, the dandelion is also a stalwart weed. Young plants have oval-shaped leaves, which hug the ground closely enough to escape damage from lawnmowers. The seedling grows very slowly at first, for the plant is busy storing energy in a vertical, extremely well-anchored taproot. Once the taproot is in place, the plant can endure having its head removed several times. It recovers by sprouting new leaves from the upper sections of the root.

Plants more than a few months old develop arrow-shaped leaves with numerous pointed lobes along the edges. Depending on the age of the plants and the fertility of the soil, leaves may be 3 to 10 inches long. They often show purplish color near the plants' centers, where the leaves emerge from the crowns. Young leaves are edible and have a mild, spinachlike flavor when harvested in early spring, before the flowers have formed.

Dandelion flowers begin appearing in early spring and open during morning hours to bright yellow discs an inch or more across. The flowers are edible. When battered and fried, they taste like mushrooms.

Within days after the flowers fade, the bare flower stalks are topped with feathery round "blowballs" made up of seeds, each with its own downy white parachute. Dandelions flower most heavily in spring but continue to flower sporadically all summer in many climates. A new flower is imminent when you can see a small green button in the plant's center.

When dandelions stop flowering, they slowly continue to produce new leaves, which arise very slowly from the plants' centers and may not be as dramatically lobed as the leaves that grew in spring. In most areas, dandelions devote most of their energy to storing up more food in their roots, thus gaining strength for the new season ahead. In warm weather, older leaves may become speckled with powdery mildew, evidenced by pale white patches on the top sides of leaves.

In cold climates dandelions die back to the roots in winter, but in mild winter areas they hold on to some green leaves year round.

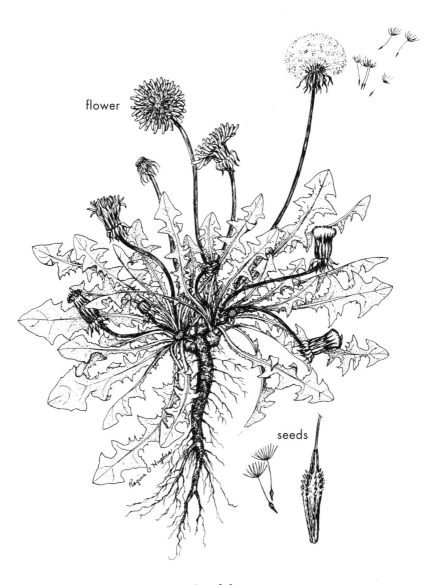

flower

seeds

Dandelion

Life cycle: Perennial
Origin: Europe
Range: North America

Flower color: Bright yellow
Height: 4–6 inches (10–15 cm)

Dandelion

Control: Dandelions survive various forms of abuse — including mowing after mowing — as long as their taproots remain intact. You can pull up very young seedlings, but plants old enough to show lobed leaves usually break off at the crown when you try to pull them.

A weeding tool called a V-weeder is useful for plucking out dandelions (see page 29). Insert the end of the tool downward alongside the root and then twist the tool to dislodge, or at least mangle, the dandelion root. Partially lift out the tool, use the forked end to grasp the upper end of the root in a stranglehold, and pry it to the surface.

A few dandelions in garden pathways are not a problem until their seeds start blowing all over your yard. If you cannot stand having dandelions in your lawn, you must be very vigilant about removing young plants as soon as you see them. Since digging them out would leave open wounds in the turf (which in turn might be colonized by other weeds or more dandelions), try cutting dandelion roots diagonally with a sharp, slender knife at least 2 inches below the surface. Then pull out the part of the plant you have severed. Fertilizing, watering, and reseeding your lawn as needed to keep it growing strong will seriously limit the opportunities dandelions find for establishing themselves.

Of course, you can always decide that you like dandelions. They are pretty, edible, and often colonize spots where other plants refuse to grow. Few weeds make happier additions to ugly ditches than the lowly dandelion. ∎

Curly dock

Rumex crispus

Yellow dock, narrow-leafed dock, sour dock

Broadleaf dock

Rumex obtusifolius

Bitter dock

Pale dock

Rumex altissimus

Water dock

Site, soil, and season: These perennial plants grow back each spring from woody taproots and usually flower in early summer to midsummer. Curly dock is found in all types of soil and can grow in acidic soil better than many other plants. Broadleaf dock is partial to moist, shady places, while pale dock seldom grows in sites that are not constantly damp, such as the edges of ponds and streams. Yet because the latter two plants produce numerous seeds, they occasionally appear in gardens, too.

Description: Curly dock is easily identified from its seedling stage until maturity. The sprouts form circular rosettes, often with maroon tinges in the center of the crown. The oblong, slightly glossy leaves often have a granular coating on their undersides. Young leaves have smooth edges.

As the plants prepare to flower, a central stem emerges from the crown, and leaves grow alternately (rather than opposite one another) along this stem. The leaves can become quite large, up to 12 inches long, and their edges become wavy and curled. The central stem terminates in large masses of small greenish flowers. At this point the plant may be between 1 and 4 feet tall. Broadleaf dock is very similar in size and growing habit, except that its leaves are not curled along the edges. Pale dock leaves are long and slender, also with no curled edges.

Dock seeds mature to reddish brown, and each one is held in a papery, brown heart-shaped wrapper. A healthy curly dock plant can produce 40,000 seeds, and the seeds have been known to remain viable for 70 years. Dock seeds can travel in manure, as they easily pass through the digestive systems of horses, cows, pigs, and sheep.

One of curly dock's redeeming characteristics is that the leaves are quite edible, especially the tender young greens. Nibbling dock in a salad is a special pleasure of early spring, for mature leaves are bitter and tough. Since dock contains a heavy dose of oxalic acid, sufferers of kidney stones should avoid eating it.

Below ground, docks grow from long, woody taproots that can reach 2 feet in length. When the top of the plant is cut off, a new growing crown can develop at the top of the root.

Control: Since dock plants usually appear as scattered individuals in gardens, they are relatively easy to control. Pull up young plants during routine weeding. Lop off the heads of any that threaten to flower in or near your garden and dig them up when you have time. Push a narrow spade into the ground close to the central crown, loosen the soil around the plant, and pull it up. As long as you remove the top 4 or 5 inches of taproot, the plant will perish and the lower section of the root will rot. ■

Family Ties

Dock is distantly related to rhubarb and can serve as a host for a rhubarb-eating pest called the rhubarb cucurlio. Sorrel (page 128) is a close cousin and often is seen in the same areas as curly dock.

seed capsule

seed

Curly dock

Life cycle: Perennial

Origin: Native to Asia, introduced through Europe

Range: Throughout the United States and southern Canada

Flower color: Green

Height: 1–4 feet (30–122 cm)

Docks

seed

Broadleaf dock

Life cycle: Perennial
Origin: Native to Asia, introduced
through Europe
Range: Throughout the United States and

southern Canada
Flower color: Green
Height: 1–4 feet (30–122 cm)

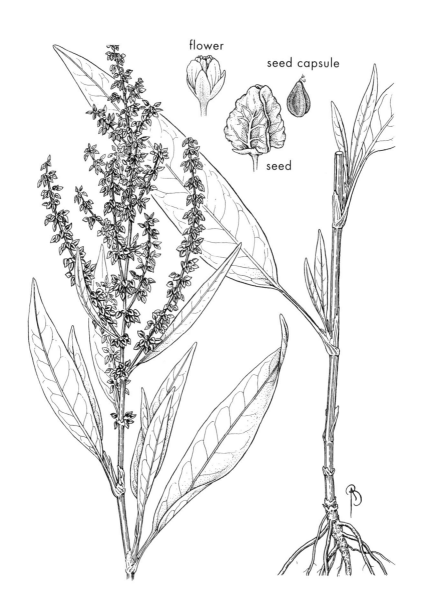

flower

seed capsule

seed

Pale dock

Life cycle: Perennial
Origin: North America
Range: United States and southern
   Canada

Flower color: Green
Height: 2–4 feet (61–122cm)

Docks

Galinsoga

Galinsoga ciliata

Frenchweed, quickweed

Site, soil, and season: Galinsoga grows best in warm weather. It is common in gardens, ornamental beds and other cultivated spots where the soil is rich and slightly acidic. Galinsoga prefers full sun or partial shade.

Description: Galinsoga seedlings are short, stocky plants with dark green leaves. The edges of the first 3 or 4 leaves are nearly smooth with pointed tips but later leaves have coarse irregular teeth all along their outer edges. Leaves grow opposite one another on the stems, and most plants develop several stems which give them a bushy look. Stems near the base of the plant are often maroon in color.

This weed is often called hairy galinsoga because all of the plant parts are covered with very fine white hairs. You will not need a magnifying glass to see these hairs on the stems, which often curve downward like little barbs. They are not prickly.

Galinsoga plants grow numerous branches and flower when they are 6 to 18 inches tall. The flowers are small yellow buttons with 5 very short white petals. Plants usually flower in flushes. Seeds from the first blossoms often mature before the last blossoms have opened. When storms knock the lower branches to the ground, they can develop roots along the stem area that touches the soil.

Control: Because of its naturally bushy habit, galinsoga becomes stronger when it is topped back, an operation that encourages stronger branching and more flowers. Hoe this weed down below the soil line or pull up small plants when the soil is wet. As the plants age, they develop a very strong, resilient root system. Dig beneath older plants before attempting to pull them from the soil. Young plants that have not developed viable seeds may be composted. ■

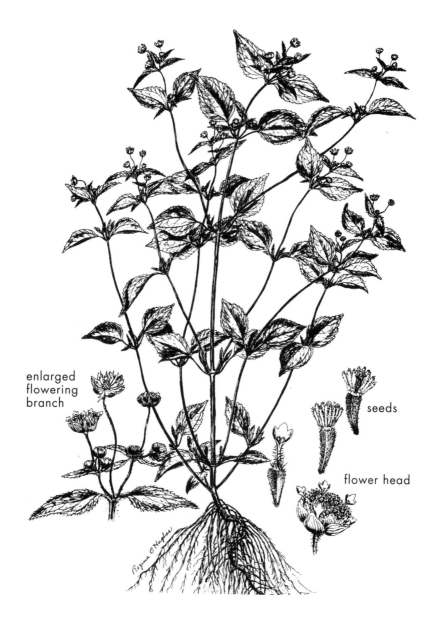

enlarged
flowering
branch

seeds

flower head

Galinsoga

Life cycle: Summer annual
Origin: Mexico and South America
Range: North America through Zone 4

Flower color: Yellow and white
Height: 6–20 inches (15–51 cm)

Galinsoga

Wild garlic

Allium vineale

Field garlic, wild onion, crow garlic

Site, soil, and season: Wild garlic appears in winter, before other plants awaken from their winter sleep, and becomes dormant in late summer. It is not picky about soil or exposure, yet grows best in places that are not often cultivated, like your lawn. Individual plants appear in gardens and frequently pop up near small shrubs and perennials.

Description: Wild garlic is the bane of lovers of smooth lawns, especially lawns made up primarily of grasses that become dormant in winter such as bermuda and zoysia. In early fall, when nights cause these grasses to become dormant, the underground corms of wild garlic are just waking up. They slowly grow roots and tops, and by early spring they are the liveliest life forms in the lawn. When the grass starts growing in spring, the wild garlic grows faster, so you must mow often to keep everything growing at a uniform height.

Wild garlic plants smell strongly of onion. Individual leaves are slender, hollow, and would be round except for shallow grooves along their length. Left uncut, the plants can grow to 3 feet tall.

Below ground, wild garlic is anchored in place with a small bulb. If you gently dig up a bulb you will see small corms (like hard-shelled cloves) loosely attached to the outside of the bulb. When the plants are pulled up (or roughly dug) these corms are left behind to grow into next year's wild garlic crop.

Wild garlic also reproduces above the ground by developing a cluster of bulblets on a tall stem. The cluster bears flowers, though the flowers do not always develop seeds. When the bulblets fall to the ground, they develop roots and grow into plants.

Control: This plant is difficult to eradicate in lawns since the bulbs are so deep that they must be dug out. Plus, even with careful digging, the corms can be left behind in the soil. If you insist on an allium-free lawn, dig the clumps and individual plants in late spring, after the lawn has begun growing vigorously, and be prepared to replant the disturbed spots immediately with sod or grass seed that matches the rest of your lawn.

If you cannot dig plants from perennial beds without hurting culti-vated plants that grow nearby, take a knife with a long, slender blade

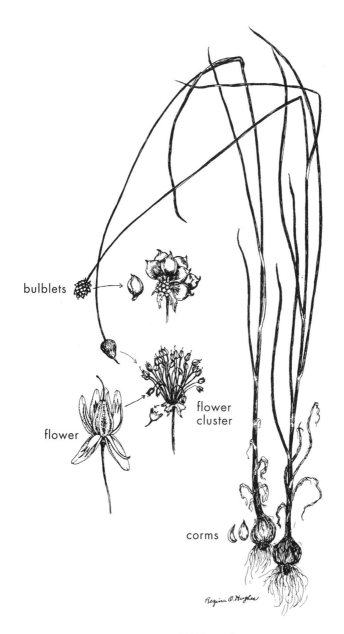

bulblets

flower

flower
cluster

corms

Regina O. Hughes

Wild garlic

Life cycle: Perennial
Origin: Europe
Range: Mid-Atlantic states and upper South; Pacific Northwest; isolated pocket in the Great Plains
Flower color: White
Height: 1–3 feet (30–91 cm)

and ram it straight down the shaft of the plant. Then twist, and pull out the severed plant part.

Another alternative is to simply tolerate this weed during its active period of growth (do mow it before it can topset bulblets). The leaves are edible, though not very tasty. In vegetable gardens, several seasons of repeated cultivation often eradicates wild garlic. ■

More Annoying Alliums

Wild garlic is called wild garlic because it produces corms similar to garlic cloves. A native cousin, *Allium canadense*, produces no cloves but otherwise could pass for a wild garlic lookalike. Commonly known as wild onion, *A. canadense* is simpler to battle because it lacks those obnoxious corms. Several other wild alliums are native to North America (especially the West Coast), but none produces the root corms that make wild garlic so persistent.

Ground ivy
Glechoma hederacea

Creeping Charlie, gill-over-the-ground, cat's foot, field balm, dollar plant

Site, soil, and season: A creeping perennial, ground ivy grows best in moist partial shade. Its blue flowers appear from March to June, sometimes longer. This weed is a common invader of lawns and flowerbeds. Since roots can form at each node (the place where leaves are attached to the stem), plants often form a solid mat. Ground ivy adapts well to cold climates.

Description: Ground ivy is a relative of mint, though the crushed leaves do not give off a clear minty fragrance. But like mint, ground ivy is a mat-forming spreader and incredibly invasive. Some people think both the plant and its flowers are pretty and welcome this weed's appearance in spring. Others battle it constantly to keep it from overtaking garden beds.

Ground ivy leaves are nearly round with scalloped edges. Numerous small plantlets grow from the wandering stems, and a small tuft of roots develops beneath each plantlet. Leaves emerge from the stems opposite one another; the stems are square rather than round.

Light purple flowers shaped like little funnels with a rounded lower lip and dark speckles on the lower petal appear in late spring, usually in small clusters. Each flower produces 4 triangular seeds.

Ground ivy spreads by seeds and by stretching its creeping stems outward 30 inches or more. When mowed, new plantlets eagerly emerge from the ground-hugging stems left behind.

Ground ivy has a long history of medicinal use for everything from curing heart disease to telling you when witches are near. If you believe in its powers, it's best to use ivy tea only externally (for washing wounds perhaps), because the leaves contain volatile oils that can be toxic. Flavorwise, ground ivy leaves leave much to be desired.

Control: I battled ground ivy for ten years in my old house and finally gave up and let part of the lawn grow as mostly ground ivy (if you think of it as a ground cover, it's an acceptable plant). To keep it from overtaking my herbs and flowers, I pulled piles of the stuff from my beds several times a year. When I moved to an ivy-less house, I made sure that no plants that moved with me hosted even a small tendril of ground ivy. It worked!

Actually ridding your yard of ground ivy is an all-or-nothing proposition. Pull up every stem you see and pile them in a sunny spot where they will dry to death. When your lawn-versus-ground ivy war results in bare spots, reseed them with a vigorous lawngrass or some other crop that will quickly occupy the spot. Continue routing out the ivy once a month all summer and again the following year. With persistence and dedication, you can gain the upper hand over this weed. ■

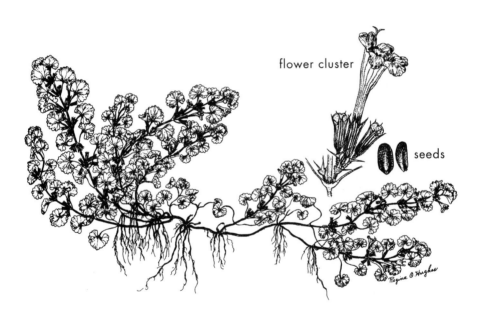

flower cluster

seeds

Ground ivy

Life cycle: Perennial

Origin: Europe

Range: Throughout much of the world; common except in far South and far

West; occasionally in Arctic Circle

Flower color: Light purple

Height: 6 inches (15 cm)

Poison hemlock

Conium maculatum

Water hemlock

Cicuta maculata

Spotted waterhemlock, European hemlock, cowbane, poison parsley

Site, soil, and season: Both of these poison plants rarely grow as weeds in gardens, yet because they are so poisonous and because they live in moist soil, their appearance in a garden environment is possible.

Anyone who spends time with plants should know these toxic cousins of parsley. You are most likely to encounter them in wet places such as low spots in pastures, wet open woodlands, or along the edges of ponds and streams. In gardens, you may find biennial poison hemlock, which sprouts in fall and forms a rosette that's similar to Queen Anne's lace (wild carrot). I have found it growing through ground cover vinca, and once in a mixed border.

Water hemlock is basically a water plant. Either hemlock may become established along irrigation ditches in dry areas.

Description: Neither of these hemlocks is an aggressive garden plant, but both are extremely poisonous. In European hemlock, the whole plant contains toxic alkaloids, but especially the leaves. Water hemlock is highly poisonous, too, especially the fleshy roots, which resemble sweet potatoes. If eaten, a small chunk of root can kill a person.

Both hemlocks often have red or purple spots on the stems, though these spots often are not present until the plant is quite mature. Yet the stem spots are the best way to tell if you are looking at an herb (such as chervil or coriander) or at poison hemlock.

As members of the carrot family, both species of hemlock tend to grow stout taproots. Perennial water hemlock plants more than 2 years old have clusters of tuberous roots just below the soil.

The leaves of the two species are quite different. European hemlock's finely divided, lacy leaves make it easy to mistake for the herb known as chervil, or perhaps an ornamental flower. It has been grown as an ornamental, for the small umbels of white flowers are quite pretty. Plants grow 2 feet tall or may reach 6 feet in some sites.

Water hemlock has pointed leaves, with each compound, 8-inch long leaf comprising leaflets 1 to 4 inches long, slightly toothed along the edges. The main stem is hollow, often streaked or spotted with purple near the base. Small white flowers appear in small irregular clusters.

Control: Neither of these hemlocks has characteristics that make it valuable. Pull them up once they are identified. Never allow them to develop viable seeds. ■

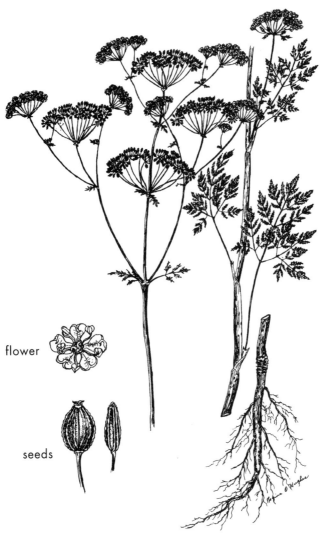

flower

seeds

Poison hemlock

Life cycle: Biennial and perennial
Origin: Europe
Range: Throughout much of North America

Flower color: White
Height: 2–6 feet (61–183 cm)

flower

seeds

Water hemlock

Life cycle: Perennial
Origin: North America
Range: In moist places and stream banks from eastern Canada to New Mexico

Flower color: White
Height: 3–5 feet (91–152 cm)

Henbit

Lamium amplexicaule

Dead nettle, blink nettle, bee nettle

Site, soil, and season: Henbit typically sprouts in fall, after the soil has been cultivated following the removal of summer plants. It grows well in partial shade or full sun and is considered an indicator of rich, moisture-holding soil.

Description: Henbit seedlings usually hold only a few leaves through winter. The leaves are generally round with scalloped edges, attached to stems that often show purple color near the ground. Both stems and leaves are studded with very tiny white hairs.

In late winter the plants begin to grow, developing pairs of leaves opposite one another on stems that often fall over and rest their elbows on the ground. Purple flowers appear by midspring in small clusters among the topmost leaves, which are seldom more that a foot high. Look closely, and you'll see a frizzy beard on the upper lip of each flower. Many nongardeners admire henbit as a pretty spring wildflower.

Control: Pull young plants from cultivated beds in late winter or destroy them through normal spring tillage. When weeding in cold soil where henbit has appeared close to pansies or flowering perennials, use a table fork to lift and twist the plants out of the soil. In lawns, pull out henbit where you don't want it or enjoy the flowers and then mow the plants down. ■

Naughty and Nice Nettles

A close cousin called spotted dead nettle *(Lamium maculatum)* is almost as common as henbit, and it's a true perennial. The flowers are similar, but spotted dead nettle is a smaller plant with a more refined growth habit. It flowers a few weeks later than henbit. Several named cultivars with white or pink variegated leaves have been selected from *L. maculatum,* including White Nancy, Beacon Silver, and Shell Pink. They make wonderful ground covers in light shade.

Henbit

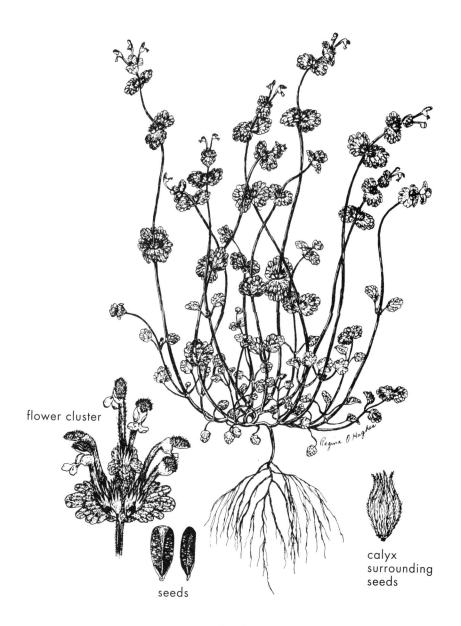

flower cluster

seeds

calyx
surrounding
seeds

Henbit

Life cycle: Winter annual

Origin: Africa and Eurasia; to North
America via Europe

Range: North America wherever winters
are mild enough to permit its survival
from fall to spring

Flower color: Purple

Height: 4–12 inches (10–30.5 cm)

Horsenettle
Solanum carolinense

Carolina nettle, bull nettle, apple of Sodom, wild tomato, devil's tomato, devil's potato, sand brier

Site, soil, and season: This perennial weed dies back to its woody roots in winter and new plants appear from midspring until frost. It is found in many different soils, in full sun or partial shade.

Description: Horsenettle is the most prickly member of the tomato family. Its leaves resemble eggplant, yet its stems are so well endowed with stickers that you should not attempt to touch it.

Where you see one horsenettle plant you are likely to see several, for this perennial weed develops brittle underground rhizomes which bud into new plants. If you mow down horsenettle plants, new ones usually pop up less than a foot from where the original plants grew.

Horsenettle plants also grow from seeds. Seedlings have oval leaves, often with purplish stems. The leaves grow alternately (rather than opposite one another) on the stem. Prickles are seldom seen on young plants, but by the time the leaf shape changes into wavy lobes, prickles develop on all stems, and usually on the main leaf vein, too.

In bloom, horsenettle plants resemble dark green eggplants, with star-shaped white or light purple 5-petaled blossoms. A few weeks after flowering, juicy yellow-orange berries appear, which gradually dry to hard wrinkled nuts. Each one contains numerous seeds.

Control: Casually digging up the plants and roots will probably leave behind bud-bearing root sections, which will develop into new plants. To get rid of a colony of horsenettle once and for all, use this procedure: Carefully dig plants from beneath with a spade, gently lifting the roots with the plants attached. Place the plant and rootball in a wheelbarrow, box, or other container before shattering the soil that clings to the roots. Pick out the root pieces and plants with a gloved hand (you never know about those prickles!) and sift through the soil with a hand rake to make sure you have gotten every piece of root. Dispose of the rhizomes and plants in a dry pile and compost them after they are thoroughly dead.

Even with careful digging, don't be surprised to see a few horsenettle plants in the area in subsequent years. Continue digging them out and mulch to make it more difficult for them to emerge from their subterranean hiding place. ∎

A Buggy Bonanza

Flea beetles often feed on horsenettle, riddling its leaves with small holes. The Colorado potato beetle likes it, too. Horsenettle also serves as host for several pepper and tomato viruses. Since its roots remain alive through winter, horsenettle fulfills the devilish function of harboring tomato-family viruses from one year to the next.

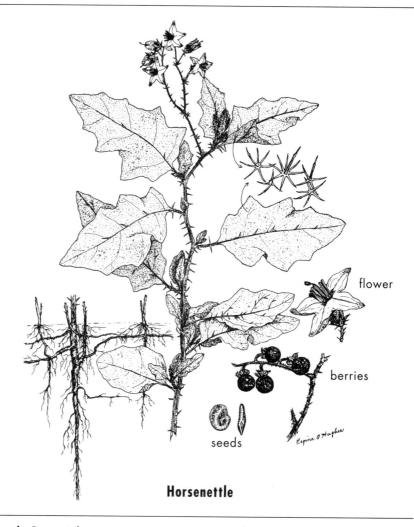

flower

berries

seeds

Horsenettle

Life cycle: Perennial
Origin: Southern United States
Range: Southern United States into Canada and westward to the Pacific Ocean
Flower color: White or light purple
Height: 6 inches to 4 feet (15–122 cm)

Jimsonweed

Datura stramonium

Jamestown-weed, thorn-apple, mad-apple, stinkwort

Site, soil, and season: A summer weed, jimsonweed has long been associated with hog pens, stockyards, and other places where the soil is rich and moist. Seeds germinate after the soil has warmed in spring and flower in late summer.

Description: Jimsonweed seedlings are large, and when newly sprouted, the leaves often show purple central veins. Later, the purple color is limited to the stems, and the leaves appear mostly green. The large, 4-to-8-inch-long leaves grow alternately on the stem and have pointed tips and 2 or 3 pointed lobes along each side. Their top sides are darker green than the undersides. When crushed, the leaves emit a rank odor.

By late summer, jimsonweed plants can reach 4 feet in height. Single trumpet-shaped flowers, 2 to 4 inches long, emerge from the joints where the leaves attach to the stems. The base of each flower is encased in a long ridged tube. When the flowers open, they are white or white tinged with pinkish purple. A subspecies bears purple flowers with purple stems to match. The flowers open at dawn and close by midday.

Flowers give way to egg-shaped seed capsules — some a full 2 inches long — that are covered with spines. Inside are numerous ⅛-inch-wide, flat, kidney-shaped seeds.

All parts of jimsonweed plants contain a potent poison called hyoscyamine that can cause hallucinations, convulsions, or death. Besides this threat, contact with the plant's sap causes a rash in sensitive individuals.

Control: Cut down young plants with a sharp hoe, cutting just below the soil line. As long as the plant has not yet flowered, compost it. Large plants should also be cut down. Use pruning shears to sever the main stem close to the soil line. Burning is often recommended as the preferred way to dispose of seed-bearing plants, but dumping them in a lake or simply allowing them to rot in a dark, wet place will accomplish the task equally well. ■

ripe capsule

seeds

leaf

Jimsonweed

Life cycle: Summer annual

Origin: Tropical Asia

Range: Throughout much of North
America except for the high deserts

of the West

Flower color: White, white tinged with
pinkish purple, or purple

Height: 2–4 feet (61–122 cm)

Lambsquarters   *Chenopodium album*

White goosefoot, pigweed, fat hen, mealweed, frost-blite, bacon-weed

Site, soil, and season: Lambsquarters is one of the most common summer garden weeds, with new flushes of seedlings often appearing after every rain. The plants are killed by frost but can adapt to almost any type of soil and site except for deep shade.

Description: In young lambsquarters seedlings, the first few leaves often show some maroon on their undersides. Later, the leaves look dusty white beneath, as if they were dusted with white cornmeal. Most of these white granules fall off as the leaf matures. Leaves develop alternately (rather than opposite each other) on the stem, are between 1 and 3 inches long, and are remarkably smooth with slightly toothed edges. Leaves become smaller and more oblong when the plants are ready to flower.

The upright plants grow very quickly and usually flower when they are between 2 and 5 feet tall. If decapitated at a young age they develop into shorter, bushier plants, but when crowded, lambsquarters tends to grow straight up.

The stems of this weed are hairless, with shallow grooves and often with red, pink, or light green streaks. Lambsquarters flowers hardly look like flowers at all, for they are green and lack petals. The flowers appear in green clusters where leaves join the main stems and at the growing tips of the topmost branches.

Mature seeds are small, shiny black discs. A scrawny lambsquarters plant can produce 5,000 seeds, while a big healthy one can leave behind 500,000. When buried so deep that they cannot germinate, lambsquarters seeds will wait patiently for many years — just in case you come along with a shovel or tiller and give them a ride to the surface. And, though most weed seed must be right at the soil's surface to germinate, lambsquarters seeds will sprout when covered with 2 inches of soil or when barely covered at all.

Control: Young seedlings are easy to kill by hoeing them with a sharp hoe. They have a knack for sprouting very close to the stems of crop plants, and you will need to pull these by hand. Keep in mind that additional plants are likely to appear following rains, so plan to re-weed every 3 weeks or so.

If lambsquarters is a common weed in your garden, your soil seed bank is probably rich with its seeds. Several years of close control will reduce your problems, provided you never make exceptions and allow mature seeds to drop to the ground, replenishing the supply of seeds in the soil.

Do not compost mature plants for the seeds will likely survive the composting process. Instead, dispose of them in a dank, shady spot where any seeds that do sprout will fail due to lack of sunshine. ∎

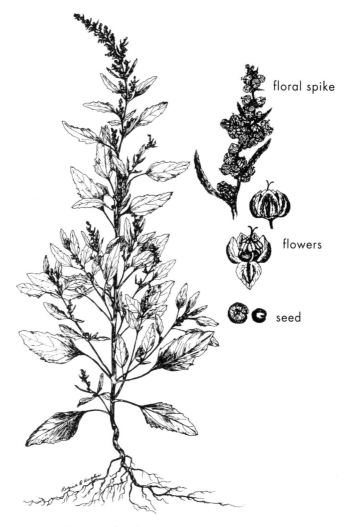

floral spike

flowers

seed

Common lambsquarters

Life cycle: Summer annual
Origin: Europe
Range: Throughout most of North America

Flower color: Green
Height: 2–5 feet (61–152 cm)

Prickly lettuce

Lactuca serriola

Compass plant, prickly lettuce, horse thistle, wild opium

Site, soil, and season: Prickly lettuce grows in rich or poor soil and can tolerate acidic conditions. In most areas, plants begin life as spring seedlings and begin flowering in midsummer. New plants continue to appear until fall.

Description: Young seedlings hug the ground, stretching out several long, narrow leaves in a loose spiral pattern. As the plants mature, a central stem elongates and may show flower buds when it is less than 6 inches high. However, most plants grow 3 to 5 feet tall before they flower. In good soil, they may get even taller before being blown over by a storm.

The main stem of prickly lettuce is hollow. When broken open, the leaves bleed a bitter white juice. Supposedly the leaves of this plant point north and south (hence the name compass plant), but if you depend on wild lettuce to tell these directions you will remain lost forever.

Prickly lettuce leaves are changeable in shape. On robust young plants, they are long and irregularly lobed, and the wavy edges are studded with numerous spines. These prickles look foreboding, but they're fleshy and do not penetrate the skin. Leaves may be as long as 10 inches, with spines along the central rib on leaf undersides. Atop, the leaf vein may be white, green, or purplish. The base of each leaf usually clasps around the main stem to form a little bulge. When the plant has grown tall and is preparing to flower, the leaves become smaller and less lobed.

Prickly lettuce flowers look like little dandelion blossoms (though of course they are several feet up in the air). Plants develop hundreds of flowers, but only a few open at a time. It's not unusual for plants to show one or two partially opened flowers, some unopened buds, and some fluffy mature seed heads all on the same day. Each dark brown seed comes loose from the mature flower with a parachute of downy white hairs at the upper end. The plumed seeds can travel long distances on the wind.

Prickly lettuce is similar in appearance to common sowthistle (see page 130), another member of the chicory tribe. However, sowthistle is more likely to grow as a winter annual and usually flowers several weeks before wild lettuce. Sowthistle prickles are sharper than wild lettuce prickles, too.

Control: Because prickly lettuce is such a prolific seed producer, do not allow it to flower in or near your garden. When the plants are small they are easily killed by pulling them up or by slicing them with a hoe just below the soil's surface. Older plants also may be cut down by cutting them low enough so that the top of the taproot is sliced away. Stumps left behind above the soil line can sprout new branches. ∎

True Blue Lettuce

Wild lettuce has a perennial cousin, *L. pulchella,* that's harder to handle than regular wild lettuce. Commonly called blue lettuce, the perennial form has similar leaves that also bleed milky white juice, yet below ground it's a much more aggressive plant. Blue lettuce has creeping roots that help it form colonies, and it also produces lots of seeds. A native to the western grasslands, blue lettuce can be a difficult weed in any cultivated space.

You can tell the difference between wild and blue lettuce by looking for prickles (blue lettuce has very few) or waiting for the plant to flower. Blue lettuce blossoms are pale blue or violet rather than yellow. To control blue lettuce, dig up seedlings and mature plants and dispose of them in a dry pile.

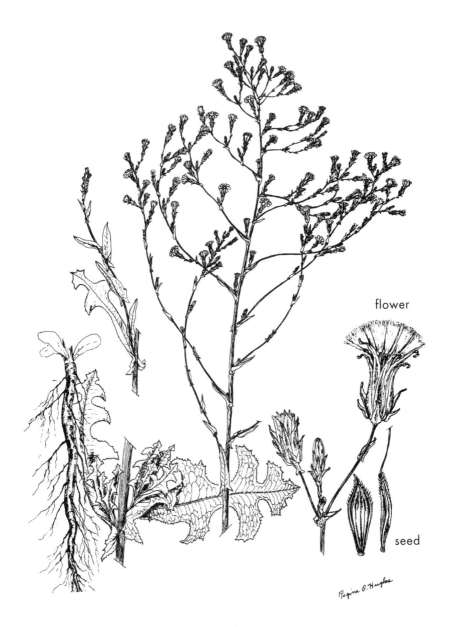

flower

seed

Prickly lettuce

Life cycle: Annual, winter annual, or
  biennial
Origin: Europe
Range: Throughout much of

North America
Flower color: Yellow
Height: 3–5 feet (91–152 cm)

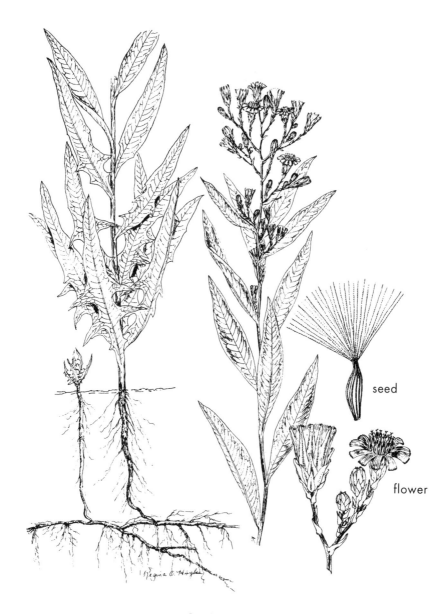

seed

flower

Blue lettuce

Life cycle: Perennial
Origin: Western grasslands
Range: Western half of North America

Flower color: Pale blue or violet
Height: 1–4 feet (30–122 cm)

Common mallow

Malva neglecta

Dwarf mallow

Malva rotundifolia

Cheeseweed

Site, soil, and season: Weedy mallows grow as a biennials where winters are mild enough for the plants to survive. In colder climates they are annuals. Typically, the seeds sprout after the garden has been cleaned and cultivated in fall, and the plants flower the following summer. Mallows grow in many types of soils and prefer full sun or partial shade.

Description: The leaves and habits of weedy mallows are quite similar to their cultivated cousin, the hollyhock. When plants are young, they appear as small, loose rosettes with only a few medium green roundish leaves attached to the plant base by long stems. In spring the stems become longer and more numerous, often spreading out over the ground in a loose mound. Leaf shape is circular, similar to bedding geraniums. The leaves are slightly hairy, and are 1 to 3 inches across.

By the time the plants are ready to flower, common mallow may reach 2 feet in height, but the less frequently seen dwarf mallow only grows half that tall. Mallow flowers look like tiny single hollyhock blooms, borne singly or in small clusters of 2 or 3. They are white or pale pink in common mallow, or pale blue to white in the dwarf form. With either mallow, you will have to look down into the plant to see the blossoms, for they are usually hidden by the foliage. The Weed Science Society of America considers both plants to be *M. neglecta.*

When the flowers fade, the plants develop seed pods shaped like flattened discs. These seedpods are edible when green, and have a crisp texture and slightly sweet flavor. As the seedpods mature, they shrivel and break into many seed-bearing segments. At this point the seedpods look like wheels of cheese scored into wedges, hence the nickname cheeseweed.

Control: Large mallow leaves shade out other plants, which can be a blessing and a curse. Allowing them to grow until you need the space for something else may help control other weeds that attempt to grow in their shadows.

Mallows are anchored in place with a thick taproot that is not very deep. Pull plants when soil is wet, and they slip right out. Mature plants are harder to pull, so remove them before they reach full size. As long as the plants do not hold mature seeds, dispose of them in your compost, or chop them as use them as mulch around other plants.

Cultivated Cousins: Mallow is closely related to garden hollyhocks. Other famous relatives include cotton, okra, and hibiscus. ■

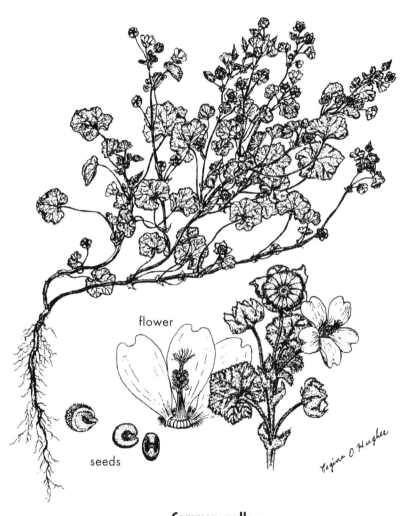

flower

seeds

Common mallow

Life cycle: Annual or biennial

Origin: Asia into Europe

Range: Throughout much of the United States and Canada; very common in upper Midwest and Appalachian Mountains

Flower color: White or pale pink or blue

Height: 2 feet (61 cm)

Milkweed

Asclepias syriaca

Silkweed, cottonweed

Site, soil, and season: Milkweed is most common as a roadside plant, but can also become an invasive visitor in the garden. Its normal habitat includes dry slopes and the edges of woodlands.

Description: No other weed rises from the ground on a single brown stem and develops pairs of oblong leaves, 4 to 8 inches long, which have smooth upper surfaces and undersides covered with a downy fuzz. If you break open the main stem, it will bleed a milky juice.

When they plants are nearly grown, clusters of fragrant white or pink flowers emerge from the stem on slender spikes. A few weeks later, unusual teardrop-shaped seedpods, covered with spines, develop in joined pairs. When these seedpods dry to brown, there is a surprise inside waiting for you. Many flat brown seeds drift out when the pods open, and each one is equipped with its own silky tuft of hair.

Below ground, milkweed plants grow from thick tuberous roots which often branch into a T shape a few inches below the surface. The horizontal legs of the T help the plants to spread. You may be able to find small buds on the roots if you carefully dig them up.

Control: With milkweed, it's essential to get to the root of your problem. Unless you can't stand the plants, allow them to grow until they are at least a foot tall and then carefully dig them up, taking as much root with you as you can get. Start digging a foot out from the plant's base and gradually work inward. If milkweed plants have formed a clump, start from the outside of the clump and move inward.

If the milkweed plants are too numerous to dig, mow them down once a month all summer, and dig the remaining roots in fall.

Never rototill over a place that has been infested with milkweed, or you may spread viable bits of root throughout your garden. If you like the sweet-smelling flowers, allow the plants to grow to flowering size before you chop them down and dig up their feet. Do take care not to let plants drop mature seeds in your garden. ■

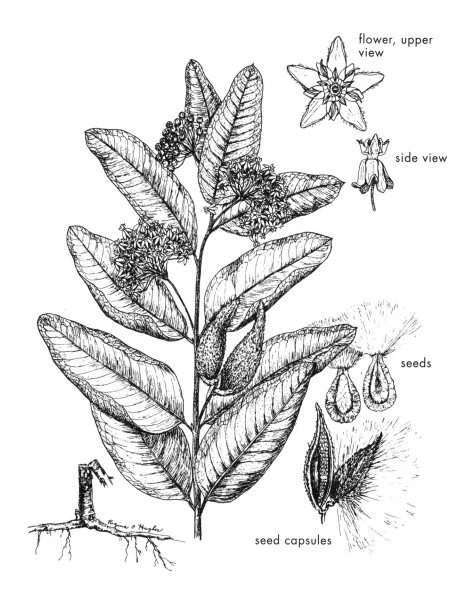

flower, upper view

side view

seeds

seed capsules

Common milkweed

Life cycle: Perennial
Origin: Eastern North America
Range: East Coast westward to Oklahoma, the Dakotas, and parts of California, and northward into eastern Canada
Flower color: White or pink
Height: 2–6 feet (61–183 cm)

Black mustard
Brassica nigra

Indian mustard
Brassica juncea

Wild mustard
Brassica kaber

Field mustard, charlock, field kale, kedlock

Site, soil, and season: The mustards are winter hardy from Zone 6 southward, where they usually grow as winter annuals. Farther north, they sprout in early spring and come into bloom in early summer. Mustard weeds grow best in cool weather and like sunny spots or partial shade. They also appreciate good garden soil.

Description: All of the weedy mustards look very much alike. As sprouts, they could be mistaken for radishes, but by the time the plants have 4 true leaves it becomes obvious that they are something else. As weeds, wild mustards and Indian mustard are the most common species.

The leaves of all three species are slightly hairy, but each has a different shape. The lower leaves of black mustard usually have two small leaflets set apart at the bottom of each leaf, with the larger part of the leaf having rough edges and a pointed tip. Indian mustard appears similar, though the leaves tend to be more irregular in shape. Wild mustard has irregular lobes all along the bottom half of the leaf, but the base of the leaf is not so clearly divided into leaflets.

As the plants become older, the leaves of Indian and black mustard become smaller and smoother, and the lobes disappear. Fat taproots develop below the soil line. Wild mustard leaves also become smaller as the plants prepare to flower.

In flower, the three mustards again look alike and stand between 2 and 4 feet tall. Nearly leafless flowering branches appear at the tops of the plants and hold clusters of 4-petaled yellow flowers at their tips. After the first flowers are fertilized (often following visits by foraging honeybees), the flower stems elongate and more flowers form at the tips. Seedpods appear growing alternately (rather than opposite each other) from the stem while the plants are still in flower. You can see the seeds swelling inside the pods, which resemble miniature green beans. With Indian and wild mustard, the tips of the pods often appear shrunken and have no seeds, while the pods of black mustard fill almost to the tip.

Mustards

The seeds of black mustard can be made into edible mustard, but the mustard you buy is of a different species, known as white mustard (because of the color of the seeds). Weedy wild mustard has black seeds that are superpungent in comparison to the white.

The leaves of all of the weedy mustards are edible, but even the young ones are spicy and slightly bitter. The green, unopened flower buds are milder in flavor and considered by some a great delicacy.

Deter Bugs with Wild Mustard Tea

Teas made from the leaves of wild mustard can be used in the garden as a deterrent to egg laying by cabbageworms, cabbage loopers, and even Colorado potato beetles. Steep wild mustard leaves in boiling water until cool, drain, and spray on cabbage, broccoli, and other cultivated brassicas before pests find them and lay eggs. Wild mustard tea is not an insecticide, but it can be a strong deterrent to egg laying by the moths whose larvae become leaf-eating pests.

Control: Pull up plants as soon as you identify them and toss them in the compost heap or lay them on the ground to dry into mulch. All of the mustards die quickly when hoed in dry weather.

If wild mustard is not in your way, you can let it grow and flower and use it as a habitat and food plant for early season beneficial insects. If aphids congregate on your mustard weeds, pull the plants up before the aphids move on to cultivated cousins.

Mature Indian mustard and black mustard often develop stout taproots, so you may need to loosen them up with a digging fork or spade before you can pull them from the soil. The wild mustards can host several diseases of cabbage as well as cabbage root maggots, so rotate into a nonrelated crop after removing numerous weedy mustards from a particular garden bed. ■

seedpods

seeds

Regina O. Hughes

Black mustard

Life cycle: Winter or spring annuals
Origin: Europe and Asia
Range: Throughout the United States and
southern Canada

Flower color: Yellow
Height: 2–4 feet (61–122 cm)

flower

seed-
pods

seed

seedling

Indian mustard

Wild mustard

Life cycle: Winter or spring annuals
Origin: Europe and Asia
Range: Throughout the United States and
southern Canada

Flower color: Yellow
Height: 2–4 feet (61–122 cm)

Black nightshade

Solanum nigrum, S. americanum

Eastern black nightshade

Solanum ptycanthum

Deadly nightshade, poison berry, garden berry, garden nightshade

Site, soil, and season: The weedy annual nightshades love both sun and shade and are most abundant in loamy soils. They grow only in warm weather and are seldom seen until the soil warms in late spring. In mild winter areas such as Southern California, seedlings begin emerging as early as February and March.

Description: Young nightshade leaves are slightly hairy, green on the upper sides and purplish below, with purplish stems. The oval-shaped leaves become dark green and develop toothed edges as the plants mature. In early summer, the plants branch out and often hug the ground during their early growth. They then shoot upward, becoming 1 to 2 feet tall, just before they begin flowering. By then the purple tint has disappeared.

The flowers look almost exactly like miniature potato or pepper flowers. Blossoms look like 5-pointed white stars with yellow stamens and are less than ⅓ inch across.

After flowering, the plants produce berries, ⅜ inches across, which are initially green and usually borne in twos and threes on the ends of slender stems. They ripen to dull black and resemble wild huckle-berries. These berries can contain high concentrations of solanine, the poisonous substance found in green potatoes. Eating the green berries can make you very sick, causing paralysis or even death. The potency of the ripe black berries is extremely variable, and nonpoisonous edible cultivars have been selected. These are the plants advertised as wonderberries or garden huckleberries.

Control: Hoe or pull up young plants before they develop ripe berries, for each berry contains between 15 and 60 seeds, and a robust plant is capable of producing up to 800,000 seeds.

Research Roundup

Several studies have found that weedy nightshades reduce tomato yields, especially when they grow alongside adolescent tomatoes that are just beginning to bloom. If unrestrained, nightshade grows faster than tomato and steals sunshine that the tomatoes need to grow.

When gardening in soil that is heavily infested with nightshade seeds, avoid cultivating soil after your crop plants have been planted — mulch instead. Nightshade seeds that are buried more than ¾ inch below the soil surface will not germinate. Because of this shallow emergence, you will probably see more nightshade weeds if it rains right after soil is cultivated. Dry soil also inhibits germination. ■

Close Relatives

Horsenettle *(Solanum carolinense)* is a prickly relative of black nightshade often seen in gardens (see page 82). Other cousins include tomato, potato, pepper, and eggplant. Black nightshade can serve as a host for many of the insects and diseases that affect these vegetables.

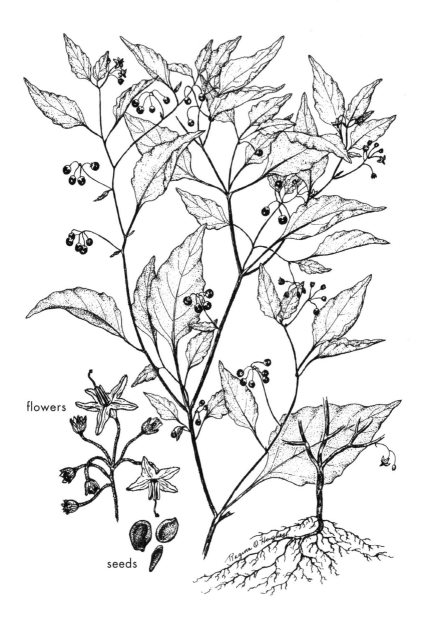

flowers

seeds

Black nightshade

Life cycle: Summer annual
Origin: Europe and Asia; some forms native
Range: Western states

Flower color: White
Height: 1–2 feet (30–61 cm)

Nightshades

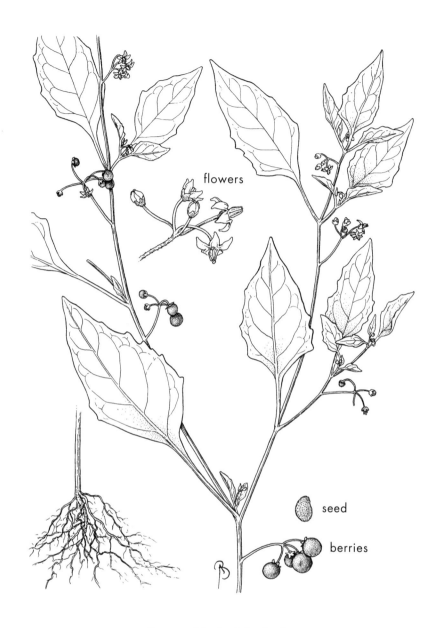

flowers

seed

berries

Eastern black nightshade

Life cycle: Summer annual
Origin: Europe and Asia; some forms
  native
Range: North America east of the

Rocky Mountains
Flower color: White
Height: 1–2 feet (30–61 cm)

Pepperweed

Lepidium virginicum

Poor man's pepper, peppergrass, bird's pepper, tongue grass

Site, soil, and season: Pepperweed likes to grow as a winter annual, sprouting in fall and coming into flower the following spring. Where winters are severe it grows as a spring annual. Pepperweed is partial to dry soils but will make itself at home just about anywhere that receives at least a half day of sun.

Description: This weed begins life as a tiny rosette in fall, and maintains that form all through winter. It is a small weed, usually only 2 inches across during its rosette period. The early leaves have longish stems, with 2 small deeply cut lobes near the base of each leaf beneath the larger oblong leaf section. Seedlings resemble those of shepherd's purse (page 123), but are not as compact and have longer leaf stems.

In midspring, the rosette gives way to a central upright stem that branches, develops small oblong leaves without notched lobes, and begins to flower. The flowers are always at the tips of the branches, in clusters of a dozen or more. The petals are white or greenish white, and the plants stay in flower for several weeks. All the while, the branches grow longer, eventually making the plants a foot tall. Beneath the open flowers, you can see little seedpods forming. The seed capsules are nearly round in shape, flat, and clearly divided down the middle. When mature, each capsule contains 2 yellow-orange seeds.

You can also get to know pepperweed through its taste and smell. If you crush a plant, its odor is strong and pungent. The flavor of the leaves is quite peppery. The most common species is *L. virginicum; L. densiflorum* is more common in the West.

Control: Pepperweed is very easy to pull up, after which you might compost the plants. If this weed grows in your lawn, simply mow it down before the seeds are mature. ■

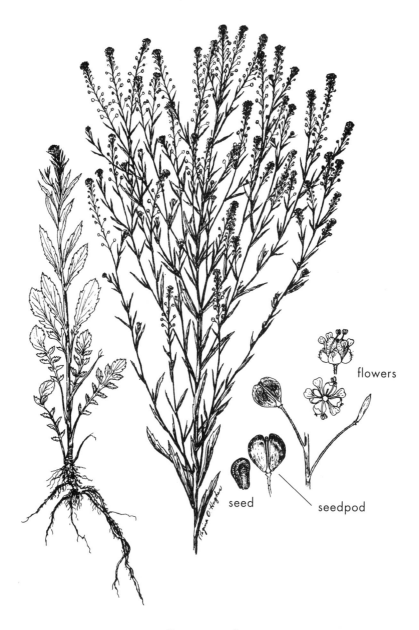

flowers

seed

seedpod

Pepperweed

Life cycle: Winter annual or annual
Origin: Eastern United States
Range: Throughout the United States except in the desert Southwest; West

(green-flowered pepperweed)
Flower color: White or greenish white
Height: 6–18 inches (15–46 cm)

Redroot pigweed
Amaranthus retroflexus

Amaranth pigweed, green amaranth, careless weed

Spiny amaranth
Amaranthus spinosus

Prickly careless weed, soldier weed

Tumble pigweed
Amaranthus albus

White pigweed

Prostrate pigweed
Amaranthus graecizans

Mat amaranth, spreading pigweed

Site, soil, and season: All of the pigweeds are summer annuals that reproduce by seeds. They begin sprouting in midspring, and more seedlings appear throughout summer, usually following rains. The plants grow very rapidly in warm weather. Pigweeds like full sun and soil that has recently been cultivated.

Description: To see the family resemblance that links the pigweeds together, you have to wait until they begin developing seeds, for the seed-bearing bracts (and the seeds within) borne by each species are similar. But when getting to know the pigweeds in your garden, it's best to consider them in pairs.

First let's look at the tall pigweeds, redroot pigweed and its prickly cousin, spiny amaranth. The leaves are green, oblong with pointed ends, and the stems of very young plants often show some purplish coloring. When you pull up the plants, the root is a distinctive pinkish-red color. Young leaves of both species are edible and can be used as a summer substitute for spinach.

Spiny amaranth gets its name from the pairs of prickly spines that grow from the places where the leaves join the stems. It is not unusual to find both redroot pigweed and spiny pigweed in the same place.

When these tall pigweeds flower, the green flowers are virtually unseen, hidden within tiny green papery bracts that grow on short spikes at the tops of the plants, and from places where leaves sprout from larger stems. The spikes on spiny amaranth are slender, while those on redroot pigweed can become quite heavy, especially when the little black seeds are ripe. If you take a ripe seed head and shatter it on the ground, the black disc-shaped seeds fall out. Amaranth seeds are an edible grain. Birds eat them, too, and then leave them in your garden as a deposit in your weed seed bank.

Tumble pigweed and prostrate pigweed are much smaller than the tall pigweeds. Their leaves are less than 1 inch long, and they have many more branches. Tumble pigweed stems are whitish, hence tumble pigweed's botanical name, which translates as white amaranth. When tumbleweeds reach full size, they often break from their roots and blow about in the wind, spreading their seeds with every bump and turn.

Prostrate pigweed is like a tumbleweed that lies down on the ground. It often occurs in dry places, where it helps protect exposed soil from erosion. As long as you limit the number of plants you allow in your garden, prostrate pigweed can be used as a living ground cover. The seed-bearing bracts of tumble pigweed and prostrate pigweed are similar to those of the tall pigweeds but much smaller in size.

Control: All of the pigweeds can be put to work in the garden, though you will have jobs for only a few of the voluteers who show up every year. The rest will need to be eliminated, for they grow so fast that they can quickly overtake cultivated crops. Pull up the young seedlings and lay them on the surface to dry. Or, chop them into your compost heap while they are green and succulent.

Some gardeners find that insects — including flea beetles and blister beetles — like to eat redroot pigweed better than garden plants, so they allow a few to stand intermingled with crop plants. Soil scientists have long theorized that redroot pigweed improves the topsoil by bringing nutrients hidden deep in the soil up toward the surface — another reason to let a few pigweeds grow, at least until they enter their reproductive stage of growth.

If you merely chop off the heads of tall pigweeds, new branches will quickly sprout from the base of the plants. For mowing to be an effective control, you'll need to mow at least twice.

In the dry, windswept climates where they are most likely to be found, tumbleweed and prostrate pigweed can be left to fulfill their natural destinies as custodians of erodible topsoil until the space is needed for cultivated plants or until they flower, whichever comes first. Pull them up when the soil is wet. Compost the plants or use them as mulch. ■

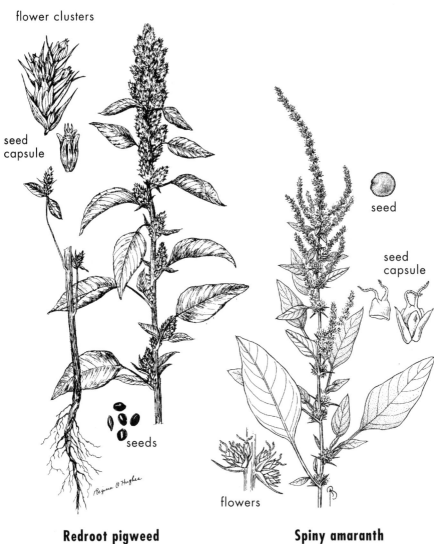

flower clusters

seed capsule

seed

seed capsule

seeds

flowers

Redroot pigweed

Spiny amaranth

Life cycle: Summer annuals

Origin: Tropical America (redroot and spiny amaranth)

Range: Throughout the United States and southern Canada

Flower color: Green

Height: Redroot pigweed, 2–6 feet (61–183 cm); spiny amaranth, 1–3 feet (30–91 cm)

seeds

flower spike

Tumble pigweed

Life cycle: Summer annuals
Origin: Western North America
Range: Southwest and Central California

Flower color: Green
Height: 1–3 feet (30–91 cm)

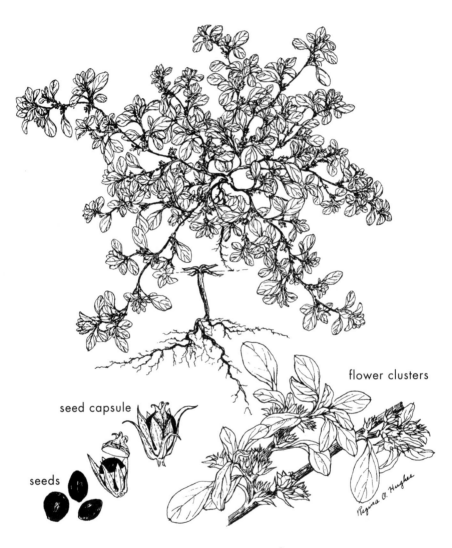

seed capsule

seeds

flower clusters

Prostrate pigweed

Life cycle: Summer annual

Origin: Western North America

Range: Many parts of North America

Flower color: Green

Height: 6–8 inches (15–20 cm)

Broadleaf plantain
Plantago major, P. rugelli

Blackseed plantain, dooryard plantain, purple-stemmed plantain

Buckhorn plantain
Plantago lanceolata

Black-jacks, English plantain, narrow-leafed plantain, rib-grass, rib-wort

Site, soil, and season: Both types of plantain are found in moist soils and prefer partial shade. Persistent perennial roots get them through the coldest winters, and they are heavy producers of seeds. Both species have been spread far and wide through contaminated alfalfa and clover seed in times past. Seedlings begin appearing in spring, with new ones sprouting all summer. Flowering time stretches from early summer into fall.

Description: Broadleaf plantain is well known to most gardeners, especially if there is a damp, compacted place where you often walk. This weed loves to grow in such places and tolerates being stepped on over and over again. The leaves grow in a low rosette from a central crown, and the stemmy parts of the leaf bases may be tinged with purple (the distinguishing characteristic of the native *rugelli* species known as blackseed). Leaves are glossy green, egg-shaped, and usually about 4 inches long and neatly divided into 5 or 7 ribs by prominent leaf veins.

When the low-growing plants have accumulated about a half-dozen leaves, 1 or 2 spikes rise straight up from the center of the crown. The little green pebbles along this spike are the flowers, which quickly transform themselves into seeds. The seeds are roughly triangular and may be dark brown or black, depending on the species.

Buckhorn plantain has thinner, strap-shaped leaves, and develops into more of a leafy tuft. In good soil (like a strawberry bed), the narrow leaves may reach 10 inches in length, though 6 inches is more typical. Leaves show 3 to 5 prominent lengthwise veins; the leaves are covered with tiny hairs.

Buckhorn plantain often develops up to 4 flower spikes, and they are topped with a pebbly cluster that looks like a pointed cylinder. Frequently a halo of little petals is seen in a ring around the lower portion of this fruiting cylinder, so that the total effect is something like a bad sombrero. The small dark brown seeds are shaped like little boats. When wet, they become covered with a mucilaginous substance that helps them stick to passing animals and aids their spread.

Control: Young plants of either species may be pulled up, but pulling becomes more difficult as the plants become larger and better anchored in the soil. Pull young plantains by firmly grasping the crown right at the soil line and jiggling it for a few seconds before you pull.

If the top of the plant breaks off, you will need a knife or weeding tool to loosen the root and pry it up. If the root is left in the ground intact, a new top will probably appear within weeks.

A colony of broadleaf plantain in your lawn tells you that the area is compacted and wet. Dig out the plantains, amend the soil with organic matter, and plant a shade-tolerant grass. ■

Plantain Soothes Poison Ivy

A few years ago, a North Carolina doctor tried an old herbal remedy to quell the itch of poison ivy, and it worked. The crushed leaves of either type of plantain, applied as a poultice, have a soothing effect on poison ivy's awful itch. It's not a miracle cure but can be especially helpful if you're far from the drug store.

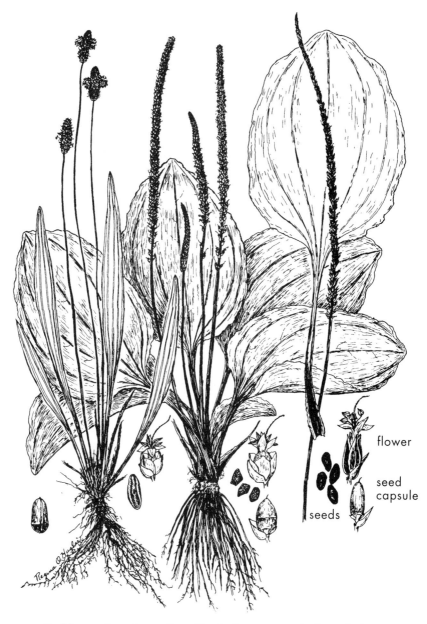

flower

seed
capsule

seeds

Buckhorn plantain   Broadleaf plantain   Blackseed plantain

Life cycle: Perennial

Origin: Northeastern United States *(P. rugelli* and others); Europe

Range: Throughout North America

Flower color: Green

Height: Buckhorn, 10–16 inches (25–40.5 cm); broadleaf and blackseed 6 inches (15 cm)

Plantains

Pokeweed

Phytolacca americana

American spinach, bear's grape, cancer root, crowberry, inkberry, pigeon-berry

Site, soil, and season: Pokeweed is partial to rich soil and often is seen near barnyards and other places where the soil has benefited from large doses of manure. Its roots are winter hardy to −10°F (−23°C), yet it grows best in very warm weather. The plant dies back to the roots in winter, and new growth emerges in midspring. Plants more than a year old have a thick, deep taproot.

Description: The young leaves of newly emerged pokeweed plants have long been eaten by country people, who gather them in spring and boil them like spinach. The large glossy green leaves, 1 to 2 inches across and 4 to 6 inches long, arise from the ground on succulent stems. The stems usually have a purplish color. The maroon color also is often present on the leaf vein on leaf undersides, right where the leaf attaches to the main stem. Poke leaves (often called poke sallet in the South) should be eaten only when very young. After the plants are a foot high, the leaves taste terrible and are poisonous to sensitive individuals.

Warm summer weather helps poke plants grow 4 to 10 feet high, depending on their age. First-year plants are comparatively small, while 3- or 4-year-old plants will tower over your head. In midsummer they produce spikes of nodding white flowers, which by fall develop into long clusters of dark purple berries. Each berry contains 10 seeds, which can remain viable for 40 years. In late fall, pokeweed leaves turn a pretty purple color.

Poke berries are useful for making inks and dyes, and making poke paintings is a long-standing tradition among country kids. Yet children should be warned not to eat the berries. The most toxic part of this plant is the root rather than the berries, but eating poke berries can cause a terrible burning sensation in the mouth. But simply playing with pokeweed berries is harmless, and the juice does not permanently stain most fabrics.

Control: Young pokeweed plants are easily pulled up when the soil is wet during routine weeding. They often appear in hard-to-reach places along fences, where you might need to chop them down with a spade rather than a hoe. Once a plant is established, chopping off the main stem at ground level will not kill it. Instead, the taproot must be dug up and allowed to dry in the sun. ■

Breaking News on Poke

Pokeweed has recently been found to contain an antiviral protein that can inhibit viruses that infect humans (including HIV) as well as viruses that infect other plants.

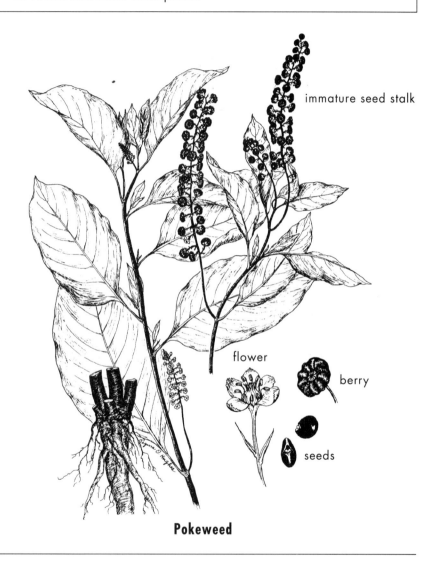

immature seed stalk

flower

berry

seeds

Pokeweed

Life cycle: Perennial

Origin: Eastern United States

Range: Northward into Ontario and southward to Florida and Texas

Flower color: White

Height: 4–10 feet (122–304 cm)

Purslane

Portulaca oleracea

Pussley or pusley, wild portulaca

Site, soil, and season: A true annual, purslane can produce seeds in as little as 40 days when weather conditions are just right. It often shows up in rich soil that receives regular water but can also grow along driveways and in ditches. Purslane seeds require warm temperatures to germinate, so seedlings show up late, after spring weeds have been cultivated into oblivion.

Description: No other common weed has succulent, juicy stems and leaves, which makes purslane easy to identify. Branching stems grow up to a foot long, and the stems usually have a reddish hue. They spread out over the ground and form a mat.

Yellow ¼-inch-wide flowers form at the stem tips and open only during sunny morning hours. In cool climates the plants flower continuously from midsummer onward, but in places where summers are very hot they take a midsummer break from flowering and start up again in the fall. The flowers give way to small seed capsules that contain numerous tiny black seeds. Under good conditions, an individual purslane plant can produce 200,000 seeds. Purslane seeds remain viable for many years. In one study, 88 percent of purslane seeds germinated after being buried for 5 years. Some evidence suggests that purslane seeds are killed when they pass through the digestive systems of horses and cows but not those of pigs or sheep.

On the plus side, purslane is edible and quite nutritious, being loaded with Vitamins A, C, and E. Try the young shoots raw in salads — expect a spinachy, earthy taste. When cooked, purslane gives off a certain slime, like that of okra, which many people refuse even to sample. As the plants get older, their edibility goes downhill.

Control: Since purslane is such a prolific seed producer, the most important aspect of controlling it is to prevent the plants from dropping seeds. Purslane is not difficult to pull up or hoe down, but it's important that the plants not be left in a situation where they might take root. Also keep in mind that purslane plants can continue to ripen immature seeds after they have been pulled up.

That being the case, enjoy nibbling at your purslane while it's young and then get rid of it. Chop up mature plants with a spade or machete before composting them or chop them and allow them to dry in the sun (the succulent leaves dry very slowly).

Cultivated counterparts: Purslane's delightful cousin, known as portulaca or moss rose *(Portulaca grandiflora)*, is a wonderful annual for warm, sunny spots. Some strains of weedy purslane have been selected and refined for growing in hanging baskets. ■

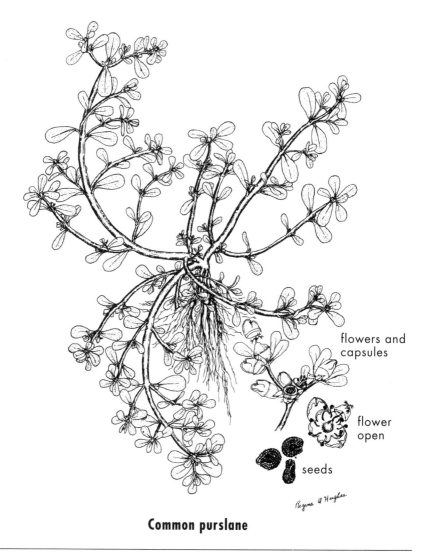

flowers and capsules

flower open

seeds

Regina O Hughes

Common purslane

Life cycle: Summer annual
Origin: Western Asia, through Europe
Range: Throughout the United States and southern Canada

Flower color: Yellow
Height: 1 foot (30 cm)

Common Ragweed

Ambrosia artemisiifolia

Bitterweed, blackweed, hayfever weed, hog weed, mayweed, wild tansy

Giant Ragweed

Ambrosia trifida

Horse weed, kinghead, tall ambrosia, wild hemp

Western Ragweed

Ambrosia psilostachya

Perennial ragweed

Site, soil, and season: Both common ragweed and giant ragweed are summer annuals that sprout following the first warm spring rains. Their pollen is the main cause of late summer hay fever. Ragweeds grow in many different soil types, and prefer full sun or partial shade.

Description: Common annual ragweed and Western ragweed have similar leaves, which grow opposite from each other along a straight stem. The leaves are finely divided into symmetrical lobes, which gives them a ferny appearance. In young plants, the base of the stem may be slightly brownish, while the rest of the stem is green. Fine white hairs grow from the upper portions of the stem, where new leaves are attached, and along the tops of the leaf veins near the stem. When crushed, ragweed leaves give off a distinctive, slightly floral odor.

Annual ragweed plants grow as individuals 1 to 4 feet high, while Western ragweed often appears in clumps with the tallest plants about 2 feet high. Western ragweed also grows horizontal roots underground, and new plants arise from the root buds.

Giant ragweed leaves are quite different from common ragweed. In giant ragweed, each leaf is divided into 3 or 5 pointed lobes, which often droop slightly. It is a much larger plant altogether, often reaching 10 feet in height in moist, fertile soils.

In late summer, all of the ragweeds develop long, flowering spikes studded with hundreds of tiny green bell-shaped blossoms. They produce clouds of pollen, followed by thousands of seeds. Giant ragweed can produce 5,000 seeds per plant. All ragweed seeds have several small spikes on one end which enable them to hitch rides on people and passing animals.

Control: Both annual and giant ragweed are easy to pull up when they are young, but become more difficult as they mature and the lower stems become somewhat woody. If you attempt to pull older plants from dry soil, they may break off just above the soil's surface, and new stems will grow from the nub left behind. Pull ragweeds when the soil is wet and compost them. They are also easily controlled with regular hoeing. When crop plants are established and the soil is warm, mulch to discourage late emergence of ragweed seedlings.

Dig out Western ragweed, for roots left in the soil quickly grow into new plants. Allow the plants to dry before composting them. Never compost ragweed plants that carry mature seeds, for many of those seeds may survive and show up in your garden the following season.

Dry weather can assist in the control of ragweed, for this weed thrives when water is abundant. In a dry summer, frequent mowing can stress ragweed to death. ■

Ragweed on the Wind

Two characteristics are shared by many weeds: They are pollinated by wind, and they have inconspicuous flowers. All of the grassy weeds are wind pollinated, as are docks, lambsquarters, pigweed, the plantains, ragweeds, and many other pesky plants. Since they do not need insects to spread pollen about, they often produce copious amounts of the stuff — a sure way to make sure there is enough to go around.

As any hay-fever sufferer will notice (with a sure degree of horror), ragweed produces so much pollen that it often can be seen leaving the plants in clouds. Although it's small comfort to the summertime sneezer, ragweed does this for a reason: Its flowers are virtually upside down, so to ensure that each one receives pollen, a great deal of pollen must be manufactured and released. Bless you!

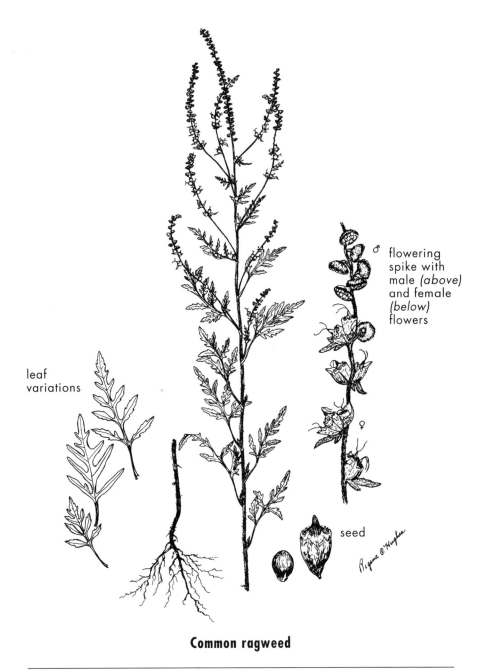

leaf
variations

♂ flowering
spike with
male *(above)*
and female
(below)
flowers

♀

seed

Regina O. Hughes

Common ragweed

Life cycle: Annual

Origin: North America

Range: Throughout North America

Flower color: Green

Height: 1–4 feet (30–122 cm)

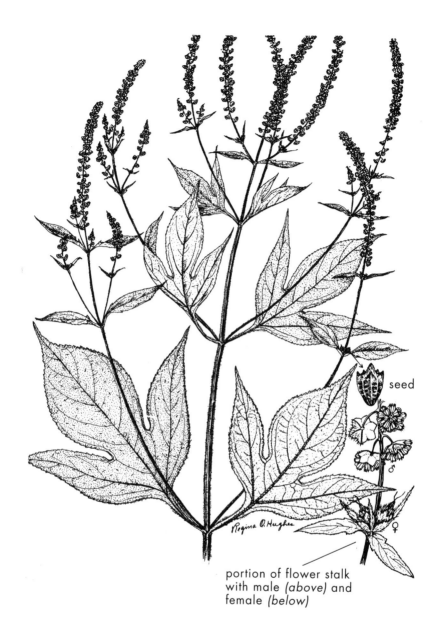

seed

portion of flower stalk
with male *(above)* and
female *(below)*

Giant ragweed

Life cycle: Annual
Origin: North America
Range: Most of North America except
    desert Southwest

Flower color: Green
Height: 4–10 feet (122 cm–3 m)

Ragweeds

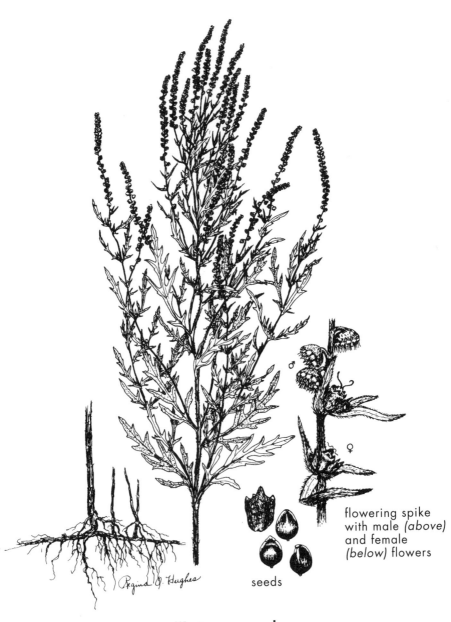

seeds

flowering spike
with male *(above)*
and female
(below) flowers

Western ragweed

Life cycle: Perennial

Origin: North America

Range: Western half of North America

Flower color: Green

Height: 2 feet (61 cm)

Shepherd's purse

Capsella bursa-pastoris

Shepherd's-bag, pepper plant, case weed, pick-purse

Site, soil, and season: A hardy annual, shepherd's purse is abundant in early spring in mild winter climates, where it often grows in community with chickweed and other hardy annuals. Where winters are cold, the seedlings sprout as soon as the ground thaws. This weed grows in many types of soil, in both sunny and shady exposures.

Description: A member of the mustard family, shepherd's purse begins life as a very small seedling that quickly grows into a circular rosette the size of a quarter. The young leaves are very deeply lobed. Seedlings that sprout in fall sit through winter as small rosettes less than 2 inches across and easily survive temperatures to 0°F.

In warm spring weather, new leaves develop from the centers of the rosettes. These new leaves are not deeply lobed and are more arrowlike in shape. If you taste a leaf, it will have a peppery flavor. Slender flowering spikes with only a few widely spaced leaves on them arise from the central crown very quickly and grow 4 to 20 inches long, depending on weather conditions. In cold weather, the tiny white 4-petaled flowers develop on very short stems and open on mild sunny days. In summer or under especially fertile conditions, longer flower spikes appear.

By the time the white flowers at the tip of the spike are open, you can see the purse-shaped seed capsules lower down on the flower spike. They are small green triangles with a center crease that gives them a triangular heart shape. Few of these "purses" ever grow to more than ⅓ inch long. If left to its own devices, a single plant can produce 40,000 seeds.

Many weedy members of the mustard family look alike, but no others develop the purse-shaped seedpods characteristic of this plant. See mustards (on page 96) for closely related look-alikes.

Shepherd's purse is edible yet not very tasty and has a long history of use as a medicinal herb. Its leaves have been used in a variety of ways, including as poultices to stop bleeding and heal wounds and as teas for cleaning out the kidneys. The leaves do contain vitamin K.

Control: Hoe or pull young plants and allow them to dry slightly before composting them. Mow down plants in lawns before they can drop seeds. A few plants scattered in the vegetable garden will not necessarily harm yields, but do remove them before they drop seeds. Plants are easiest to pull up when the soil is wet.

One word of warning: Shepherd's purse serves as an alternate host for beet leafhoppers, which carry and transmit curlytop virus to beets, beans, and tomatoes. If this virus is common in your area, keep shepherd's purse under tight control. ■

How About Shepherd's Lunch Boxes?

The botanical name of this weed, *bursa-pastoris*, literally translates as shepherd's purse. The seed pods resemble the pouches that early European shepherds packed with food and carried at their waists. In more superstitious times, the common name of witch's pouch emerged from time to time.

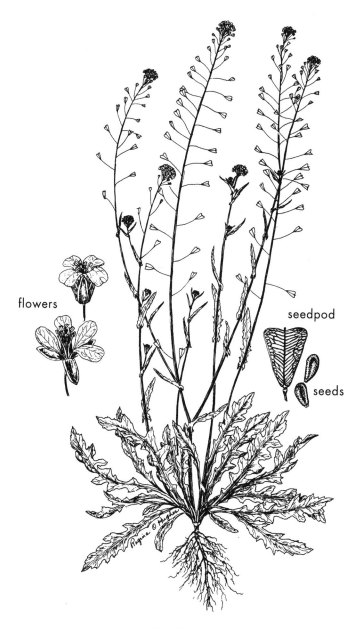

flowers

seedpod

seeds

Shepherd's purse

Life cycle: Winter or spring annual
Origin: Europe
Range: All over the world, especially in
   cool climates

Flower color: White
Height: 4–20 inches (10–51 cm)

Prickly sida

False mallow, Indian mallow, spiny sida, thistle mallow

Site, soil, and season: This summer annual often appears late in spring, for the seeds need warm soil to germinate. It thrives in full sun and will grow in many different types of soil.

Description: Despite its name, prickly sida is not prickly. Only the seeds have sharp points, which enable them to hitch rides on humans, dogs, and other animals.

Prickly sida seedlings can be identified starting with their first true leaf. Sida leaves are up to 1 inch long and ½ inch wide and are very evenly toothed along the edges. At first the leaves appear alternately (rather than opposite one another) on the main stem, but the plants soon begin to form branches where the leaves join the main stem. The stems are very tough and difficult to break.

The plants may begin flowering when they are only 6 inches high but will grow to 2 feet (or more) in moist, fertile soil. Flowers are small, yellow, and nearly hidden in the places where leaves and small stems are attached to larger stems. During midday, the petals curl down to make the blossoms look like cups.

Flowers give way to green seed capsules which dry to brown. When very dry, the seed capsules split open and 5 gray-brown seeds spill out. Each hard seed has two stiff spines at its tip, which accounts for the name of this weed.

Control: Good weed control in early summer will keep this weed from becoming a nuisance. Hoeing, hand weeding, and mulching after warm weather has begun can eliminate prickly sida from your garden.

The problem comes with gardens that are planted in spring, weeded or mulched once, and then left unkempt until fall. By then, prickly sida seeds have likely matured and rained down in large numbers. If you cannot keep a sida-infested site weeded in hot weather, at least mow between the rows. When mowed very low, prickly sida plants often cannot recover by developing new basal branches like some other weeds are able to do. ■

126   Sida

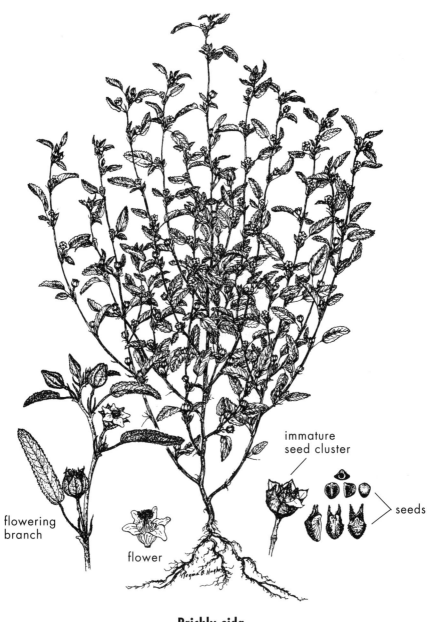

flowering
branch

flower

immature
seed cluster

seeds

Prickly sida

Life cycle: Annual

Origin: Tropical America

Range: Southeast, Midwest to northern Illinois, and westward to Oklahoma

and Kansas

Flower color: Yellow

Height: 2 feet (61 cm)

Sorrel
Rumex acetosella

Red sorrel, sheep sorrel, sour weed, sour grass, mountain sorrel

Site, soil, and season: Sorrel spreads by seeds and wandering roots. This weed can grow in very poor soils, and though it is often associated with acidic soil, it grows in slightly alkaline places as well. In mild winter climates, sorrel starts growing very early in spring and flowers just as summer gets under way. Elsewhere it grows actively from May to September. Sorrel seldom grows in heavy shade.

Description: Sorrel is a small plant, but where you find one plant you usually find many. New plants spring up from shallow spreading roots which wander about just below the soil. They frequently appear in spots that are not cultivated between fall and spring, such as the ground above hardy bulbs or the space beneath deciduous bushes (those that drop their leaves in winter) where the summer mulch has worn thin.

Sorrel is easily identified by its small size, its narrow, arrowhead-shaped leaves, and its flavor. Until they are ready to flower, sorrel plants grow only a few inches high, with each plant having fewer than a dozen leaves. The leaves have a unique sour flavor.

In preparation for flowering, sorrel plants send up a slender stem about a foot long with a few small alternate leaves on it. As the tiny flower buds develop, the predominant females take on a reddish color, while male flower buds remain green. Finally the beadlike buds burst open, a few at a time, and you can see small clusters of yellow stamens.

Sorrel leaves are edible, but you will get the best flavor from cultivated strains. If you want to eat your weeds, chop a few young sorrel leaves into a spring salad (the older ones have an unpleasantly sharp taste). To make sorrel soup or other cooked dishes from wild sorrel, blanch the leaves quickly in boiling water, drain, and then proceed to use them in any way you might use spinach.

Control: Sorrel plants tell you that the soil needs improvement, and that process alone — digging and adding compost, manure, or other soil amendments — will likely put an end to your sorrel. If sorrel colonizes the space beneath an established bush or tree where cultivating is not practical, pull out the plants when the soil is damp. Go back a month later and pull out the new ones that have emerged from bits of root left in the soil. Follow up with a good mulch of compost, rotted leaves, or straw.

Sorrel

Cultivated Counterparts: The salad herb known as sorrel is closely related to weedy sorrel but has been carefully selected and bred to produce large leaves with a more refined lemony flavor. Seed catalogs usually place the seeds on the herb page and may identify them as *Rumex scutatus* or large French sorrel. ■

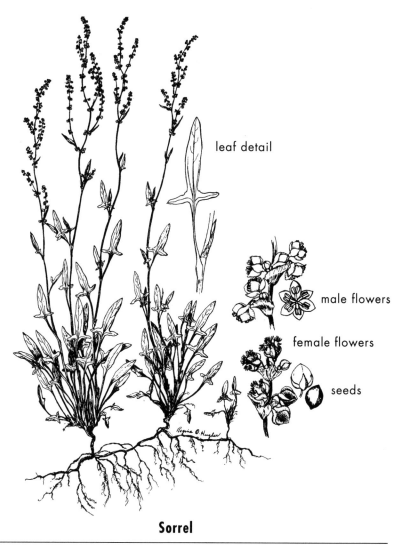

leaf detail

male flowers

female flowers

seeds

Sorrel

Life cycle: Perennial

Origin: Eurasia

Range: Throughout the United States and southern Canada, especially in the acidic soils of the eastern United States

Height: 6–18 inches (15–46 cm)

Annual sowthistle
Sonchus oleraceus, S. asper

Colewort, hare's lettuce, milk thistle

Perennial sowthistle
Sonchus arvensis

Creeping sowthistle, field sowthistle, gutweed

Site, soil, and season: Annual sowthistle grows from seeds that sprout in early spring to midspring, while the soil is still cool. Where winters are mild, the seeds can sprout in fall and grow as winter annuals. This weed needs at least a half day of sun but grows in any type of soil.

Perennial sowthistle is a terrible pest in many northern areas and has even spread into Alaska. While it does reproduce by seeds, the plant also has a hardy underground root system that spreads horizontally several inches (or even feet) below the soil. In spring, new plants emerge from buds scattered along those roots. Perennial sowthistle thrives in places that are not often cultivated and probably spread into its current range by seeds traveling along railroads. It can adapt to any type of soil.

Description: If you are looking at a thistle without a painful prickle, you probably have sow thistle. Both the annual and perennial forms are related to chicory, and both have soft, fleshy prickles along the leaf edges that bend rather than puncturing the skin. Whether annual or perennial, sowthistle flowers are yellow and resemble dandelion flowers. Also like dandelions, the seeds are equipped with little tufts of hair that enable them to fly.

The mature leaves of the different sowthistle species are shaped differently, though as seedlings they look much the same. Sowthistle seedlings hug the ground, showing no stems at all. The first leaves are dark bluish green, shaped like elongated ovals, with barely visible prickles along the edges.

By the time you really notice them, the leaves of the most common annual sowthistle *(S. oleraceus)* are long (to 10 inches) and deeply notched and are growing on upright, nonbranching plants. The end of the leaf is always triangular, but the midsection may be divided into 2 or 3 symmetrical lobes. The central vein of the leaf is lined with ¼ inch of flat green tissue. The vein becomes thicker toward the base of leaf. If you pull off a leaf and squeeze the broken vein, a white milky liquid will appear. The green lobes of sowthistle leaves taste like lettuce.

Sowthistles

Mature plants grow 2 to 5 feet tall and develop light yellow flowers at the top.

Leaves of another annual species, spiny-leafed sowthistle *(S. asper)*, are spinier and not as deeply notched but otherwise much the same as common annual sowthistle.

The leaves of perennial sowthistle are not as deeply lobed as either of the annuals, and they are usually 4 to 8 inches long. Field sowthistle leaves taste bitter but show the same milky juice as annual sowthistle. Mature plants grow 3 to 7 feet tall and develop deep yellow flowers at the top.

Annual sowthistle plants usually appear as individuals, while perennial sowthistle grows in colonies. New plants pop up from the roots of perennial sowthistle after the tops of the parent plants have been chopped off with a hoe.

Control: Do not allow sowthistle (or any other thistle) to drop its seeds in your garden. The seeds remain viable for several years, even when buried. Annual sowthistle is easily killed by hoeing it down. Just be sure to lop it off slightly below ground level so that the base of the plant is completely removed. Annual sowthistle plants also may be pulled up when the soil is wet. As long as the plants do not hold flowers or seeds, dispose of them in your compost heap.

Places infested with perennial sowthistle need to be cultivated often for 2 years. The constant disturbing of the roots is crucial to keep the colony from gaining strength. If a mass of perennial sowthistle has established itself in a ditch or waste place near your yard, mow down the plants in early summer to keep them from shedding seeds. In fall, chop away at the spot and oversow it with hardy clover, crown vetch, or another aggressive legume that stands a reasonable chance of smothering out the sowthistle. ∎

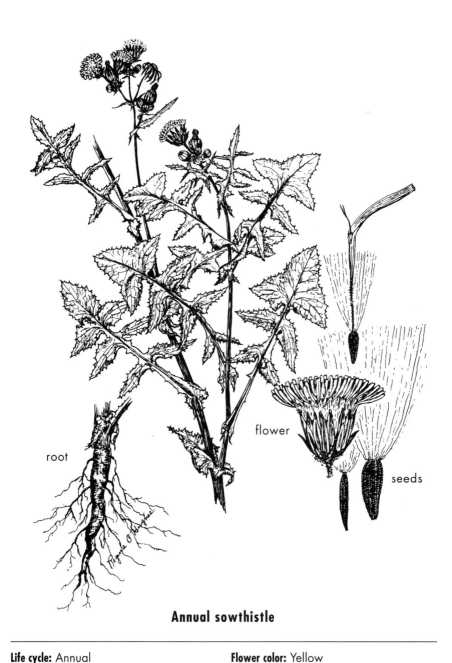

root

flower

seeds

Annual sowthistle

Life cycle: Annual
Origin: Europe
Range: Throughout the United States and
 southern Canada

Flower color: Yellow
Height: 2–5 feet (61–152 cm)

Perennial sowthistle

Life cycle: Perennial
Origin: Europe
Range: Primarily northern United States
    and southern Canada

Flower color: Yellow
Height: 3–7 feet (91–213 cm)

Sowthistles

Spanishneedles

Bidens bipinnata

Cucold

Site, soil, and season: A spring and summer annual, spanishneedles thrives in many different soils, in full sun or partial shade. Seedlings appear in early summer in soil that was cultivated in spring.

Description: Young spanishneedle plants look like ragweed seedlings (page 118), only the leaves are glossier and the stems tend to be reddish toward the base. And, while ragweed's stems are hairy, this weed's main stem is smooth. Another distinction is the way spanishneedles develops new leaves at each place where the opposite leaves join the main stem. When you pull up one of these plants, you see a smooth white taproot.

Spanishneedle plants can grow 3 feet tall, though 1 to 2 feet is more common. They develop several flowering branches. The flowers are small and yellow, with a few short yellow petals surrounding a tuft of small flowers. These quickly turn into shriveled elongated seedheads. When the seedheads dry, they release ½-inch-long brown seeds, each with three or four little spines at the end.

Control: The plants are easy to pull up when they are less than a foot tall. Allow them to dry in the sun before composting them. Mow down plants growing near cultivated spaces to keep them from dropping seeds.

Cultivated Counterparts: You may mistake these seedlings for those of *Cosmos sulphureus* (yellow or orange cosmos), which have similar leaves and coloring. Spanishneedle seedlings are more upright, while cosmos seedlings hug the ground while they are young. ■

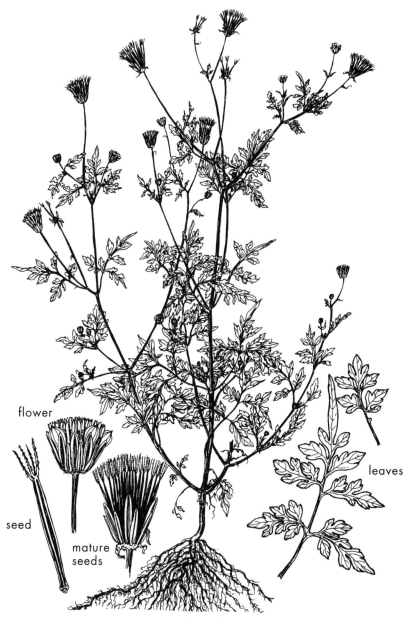

flower

seed

mature
seeds

leaves

Spanishneedles

Life cycle: Annual
Origin: Tropical America
Range: Central Nebraska and Texas to
the Atlantic Coast

Flower color: Yellow
Height: 1–3 feet (30–91 cm)

Prostrate spurge
Milk purslane

Euphorbia supina

Spotted spurge
Eye-bright, slobber-weed, stubble spurge

Euphorbia maculata

Site, soil, and season: Both types of spurge are summer garden weeds. Seeds sprout following the first warm spring rains, and more plants may appear during the summer. All are killed by fall frosts. They grow in many different types of soil, almost always in sunny exposures.

Description: Spotted spurge grows to be a stiffly spreading plant 2 feet tall and equally wide, while prostrate spurge hugs the ground and forms a low mat. The leaves of prostrate spurge are much smaller than those of its larger cousin. Otherwise the two plants are quite similar, both in terms of identification and control.

Spurge seedlings look like no other weeds. They suddenly appear as one or two reddish stems studded with a few opposite pairs of green leaves. Red coloration is quite pronounced on leaf undersides and along the slightly toothed leaf edges. After plants have 6 to 10 leaves, the leaves develop reddish blotches in their tops along the center crease. Spotted spurge plants branch into a candelabra shape, and the plants appear flat rather than bushy. Prostrate spurge forms a stiff mat over the ground. When you break open any spurge stem, a milky white juice bleeds out.

Spurges hide their tiny cup-shaped flowers in the tight places where the leaves join the main stem. The flowers of spotted spurge also dot the tips of the branches and look like tiny white specks with a small green balloon attached to them. On prostrate spurge, this little green seed capsule is easier to spot than the minuscule flowers. When ripe, each seed capsule contains 3 tiny seeds.

Control: Seedlings are easy to pull up or hoe down when small but become more of a challenge as they mature. When you try to pull a mature plant, it often breaks off at the base, and new stems may grow from any small leaf buds left behind. With large plants, loosen the soil beneath them with a hoe or digging fork before attempting to pull them up. Mow down large populations before they can drop seeds. ∎

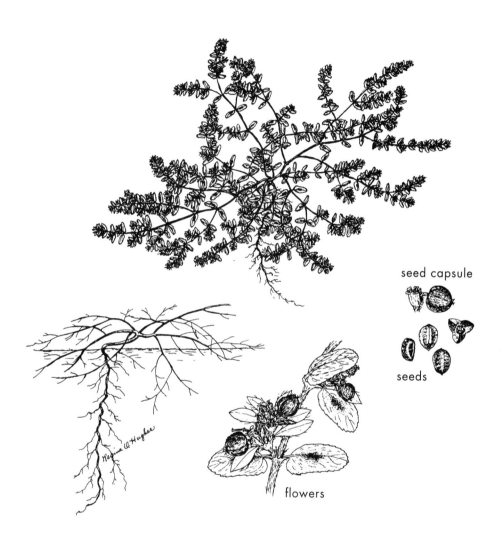

seed capsule

seeds

flowers

Prostrate spurge

Life cycle: Annual

Origin: Eastern United States

Range: Eastern half of North America and along the Pacific Coast

Flower color: White with green

Height: 2 inches (5 cm) prostrate

Spurges

Spurges Naughty and Nice

The spurge family is 1,600 species strong, and like every large family, it has its share of unsavory relatives. Some people react to contact with the white juice of all spurges by developing itchy skin blisters, but the garden variety weedy spurges are not the worst offenders. A native species sometimes grown as an ornamental, *Euphorbia marginata,* commonly known as snow-on-the-mountain, has a well-deserved reputation for making people uncomfortable. Wear gloves and long sleeves when working around these pretty yet dangerous plants.

The spurges also have a noxious cousin imported from Europe called leafy spurge *(Euphorbia esula).* This spreading perennial is very difficult to control in northern areas, where it has gained a strong foothold. Digging out every last bit of woody root is your only hope. Leafy spurge is most common in the upper midwest and mountain states.

Nice spurges include *Euphorbia polychroma* (cushion spurge), *E. amygdaloides* (purple wood spurge), and several other minor species, all of which are lovely, pest-resistant perennials.

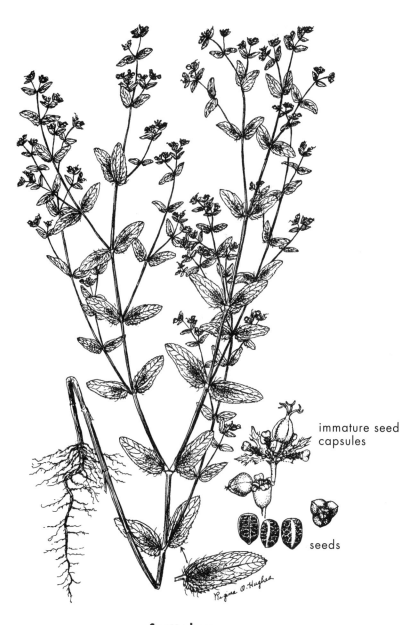

immature seed
capsules

seeds

Spotted spurge

Life cycle: Annual
Origin: Eastern United States
Range: Eastern half of North America
and along the Pacific Coast

Flower color: White with green
Height: 2 feet (61 cm)

Small stinging nettle
Urtica urens

Burning nettle, slender nettle, stinging nettle

Tall stinging nettle
Urtica dioica

Stinging nettle

Site, soil, and season: The perennial stinging nettle is dormant in winter and
grows in spring and summer. It tends to colonize damp, rich soil and
ditches, but may be encountered in neglected gardens. The annual form
can turn up anywhere, from vegetable beds to potted flowers.

Description: These plants have a bite! The hairs found along the stems and
leaf veins contain formic acid, and contact with them makes you feel
like you've been stung by a small bee. Minutes later, a small welt
appears that even looks like evidence of an insect sting. These "bites"
do not persist very long, but the discomfort is intense while it lasts.

As plants, stinging nettles look rather innocent. Symmetrical medium green pointed leaves with finely toothed edges grow opposite each
other on the stem. Where each leaf joins the main stem, there is usually
a pair of smaller leaves waiting to branch out in the event that the plant
loses its head. Left untouched, the stinging nettles tend to grow straight
up, with perhaps 1 or 2 spindly side branches emerging near the base of
the plant. The stinging hairs are easy to see and even easier to feel.

The perennial form often grows 3 to 6 feet high before it flowers,
while the annual form is mature when only 10 to 12 inches tall. The
flowers of both are similar and are so small that they hardly look like
flowers at all. Rather, they look like short bits of sticky string that have
been dipped in cornmeal. They appear all over the tops of the plants
from midsummer onward, and quickly develop into tiny gray seeds.

Tall stinging nettle develops creeping rootstocks which wander about
a few inches below the surface. Buds develop on these roots which grow
into new plants. The roots of annual stinging nettle are fibrous and
sparse, making it easy to pull up.

Control: Wear gloves when working around these dangerous plants. Long-
handled tools are also highly recommended.

To get rid of tall stinging nettle, cut the plants down and then go after
the roots. Use a digging fork to loosen the soil around the colony and
then pull up as much of the tangled root mass as you can. Spread both
roots and plants in a sunny spot to dry until dead and then compost them.

Mow down small stinging nettle or cut it down with a hoe. Make sure you cut the plants down below the soil line, or new stems will grow from the surviving root. Do not attempt to pull up stinging nettle unless you are wearing very thick gloves. ∎

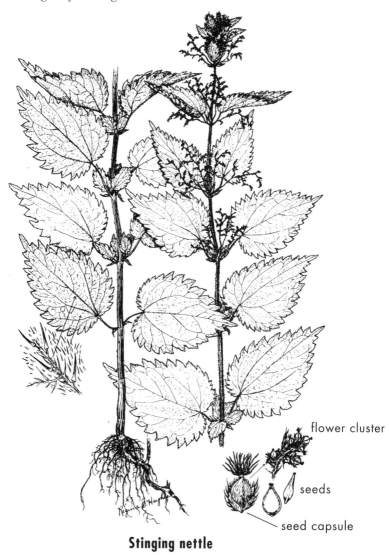

flower cluster

seeds

seed capsule

Stinging nettle

Life cycle: Perennial (tall), summer annual (small)
Origin: Eurasia; subspecies from high plains (tall), Europe (small)
Range: United States and southern Canada, more common in the East than the West
Flower color: Light green
Height: 3–6 feet (91–183 cm), tall; 10–12 inches (25–30.5 cm), small

Velvetleaf

Abutilon theophrasti

Indian mallow, butter print, velvet weed, butter weed, Indian hemp, cottonweed, buttonweed

Site, soil, and season: Velvetleaf is a warm-season annual that reproduces by seeds. In North America, it owes its success in large part to corn and soybeans, for it coexists very successfully with these two field crops. The first seeds sprout in spring, and more plants continue to appear all summer. The seeds themselves are very tough and hard-coated, and may remain viable for as long as 50 years.

Description: Velvetleaf earns its most common name because of its downy coat of soft hairs, which covers the leaves and stems. In very young seedlings the main stem is purplish at the base near the soil line, but otherwise the plants are medium green. Leaves are heart-shaped with slightly serrated edges, appear alternately (rather than opposite) on stems, and are usually about 4 inches across. Plants are very upright, and may grow as tall as 7 feet. If the tops are removed, however, they grow lower and develop branches. Underground, the plants develop very strong taproots.

Small yellow flowers only ¾ inch across appear singly where leaves join the stem. They have 5 petals which rarely open completely. After the flowers wither, round, flat-topped fruit capsules (buttons) develop, and each one contains between 5 and 15 ⅛-inch-long seeds.

Velvetleaf's greatest strength is its talent for producing lots of long-lived seeds — up to 17,000 seeds per plant. Because the seeds are so well equipped for survival, it is very difficult to withdraw them from your seed bank. In one experiment, a field that was tilled every month for four years still retained 10 percent of its initial supply of velvetleaf seeds.

Control: In vegetable gardens grown in spots where velvetleaf once had a chance to establish itself in a field crop, removing the seedlings by hand — either by pulling them up or hoeing them down — will be a season-long activity. Mulch can slow down the germination of seeds, but it's important to continue monitoring your rows all summer, even after your vegetable plants have grown large enough to shade surrounding soil. Velvetleaf can rarely be shaded out and can successfully flower and make seeds in the shadows of taller plants. ∎

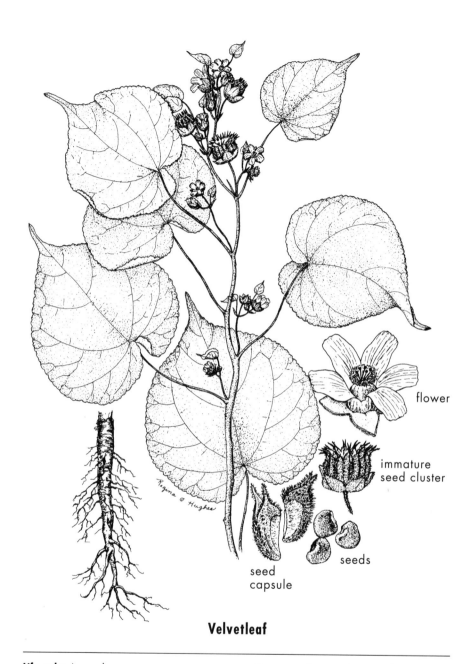

flower

immature
seed cluster

seeds

seed
capsule

Velvetleaf

Life cycle: Annual
Origin: China, India, or Asia
Range: Mild maritime climates of the
East and West Coasts of the United

States and most places in between
Flower color: Yellow
Height: 4–7 feet (122–213 cm)

Woodsorrel

Oxalis stricta

Yellow woodsorrel, sourgrass

Site, soil, and season: Yellow woodsorrel grows best in partial shade but also can live quite comfortably in the sun-baked gravel along sidewalks and driveways — at least until summer heat does it in. In most areas seeds sprout in very early spring and are ready to flower by late spring. More plants appear all summer, often snuggled into the shade of companion plants. Some plants survive winter in mild winter areas.

Description: Yellow woodsorrel looks like a small shamrock plant, to which it is closely related. The cloverlike leaves have three lobes or leaflets, with a crease down the center of each lobe. They do not have the halo of white seen in most clover leaves. You can also tell the difference between the woodsorrel and clover leaves by tasting them. Clover leaves are virtually tasteless, but woodsorrel leaves have a tangy sour flavor. They are edible and make an interesting addition to spring salads. But because of their high oxalic acid content (and robust flavor), use the leaves as a flavoring herb rather than as a mainstream vegetable.

Depending on the richness of the soil in which the plants grow, woodsorrel plants may stop growing and start flowering when they are only 3 inches high or may eventually reach a foot or more in height. The dainty yellow flowers have 5 petals, and they close up at night and during wet weather. Individual flowers last only a few days and are quickly followed by ½- to 1-inch-long green seed capsules which point upward. The capsules become ridged as they mature and explode when ripe. Each capsule releases about 50 seeds.

Sometimes when mild wet weather encourages them, woodsorrel plants develop roots along low stems that touch the ground, which adds to the longevity of individual plants.

Control: The good news about this weed is that you can enjoy it as a companionable garden plant for as long as you like and then pull it up before it drops seeds in your garden. The flowers look pretty with spring violets and other wildflowers, and the leaves offer a vibrant taste of spring. Since the seeds take 2 weeks to mature, you have plenty of time to pull up these sparsely rooted plants.

The biggest problem you're likely to have with woodsorrel is getting the plants out of tight places between pansies and other small flowers. In this situation, wind the small stems in the tines of a table fork and pull. ■

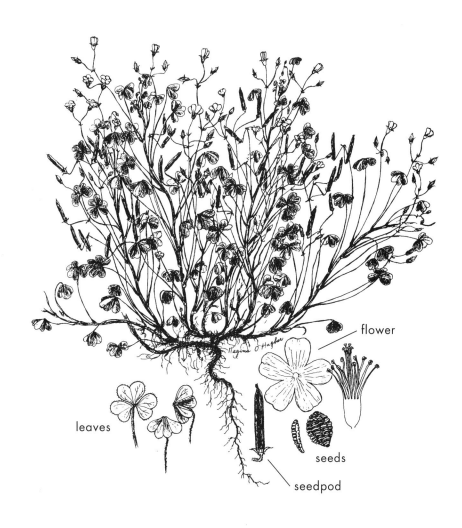

flower

leaves

seeds

seedpod

Woodsorrel

Life cycle: Perennial, often growing as a hardy annual

Origin: Europe; similar native species sometimes seen

Range: Southern Canada to the Gulf of Mexico

Flower color: Yellow

Height: 4–18 inches (10–46 cm)

CHAPTER 4

A GALLERY
OF
GRASSY WEEDS

A FRIEND WHO GROWS CUT FLOWERS hardly ever uses the word "weed" when she's talking about weed problems. Instead she speaks of the need to "stay after the grass." In Susie's long rows of zinnias, sunflowers, and dahlias, all other weeds are minor nuisances compared to the challenges posed by wild grasses. Although the world is fed by grassy plants including corn, wheat, and rice, grasses rank high as despised weeds, too. Worldwide, 10 of the 18 worst weeds are grasses.

This chapter examines 12 grasses that are common North American garden weeds. Bear in mind that in addition to producing lots of seeds and having upright architecture that enables them to fit into small spaces, many grasses exude chemicals that inhibit the growth of nearby plants (see page 10 for discussion of allelopathy). Grassy weeds are formidable adversaries for any gardener.

Annual bluegrass

Poa annua

Annual spear-grass, dwarf spear-grass

Site, soil, and season: Annual bluegrass usually grows in moist, rich soil, in either full sun or partial shade. In cold climates it is a summer annual; where winters are mild, it grows from fall to spring and dies in early summer. Although best known as an undesirable lawn grass, annual bluegrass is often an unwanted visitor in gardens.

Description: Despite its penchant for rich, moist soil, annual bluegrass is usually a lighter shade of green than other grasses. The individual leaf blades are about ⅛ inch wide and up to 4 inches long. Annual bluegrass grows into a small tuft of 3 to 5 stems; sometimes the lowest and oldest stems develop extra roots along their base.

When flowering begins, the stems stretch into wiry panicles about 3 inches long adorned with whitish "flowers." If not mowed back, these panicles eventually produce tiny brown, oval seeds. During hot summer weather, the entire plant normally dries to brown.

Control: In vegetable gardens annual bluegrass is merely annoying, but in flowerbeds it can be a chronic nuisance. Mulch where you can to keep this grass from popping up and pull out the young plants as soon as you see them. Also pull out patches in your lawn and overseed (or sod) the spot with grass that matches the rest of your lawn. Getting rid of annual bluegrass in your lawn can reduce its appearance in your garden, too.

Sometimes the plants break apart when you pull them up. If possible, use a hand cultivator to comb through the spot and remove the part of the plant left behind. As with other weeds that grow on a fibrous tuft of roots, it's easiest to pull out annual bluegrass when the soil is moist. ■

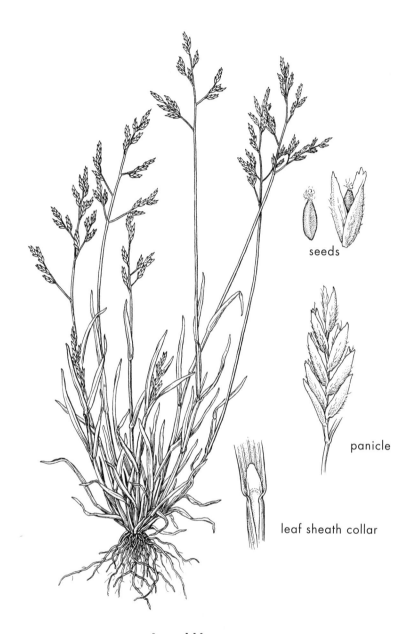

seeds

panicle

leaf sheath collar

Annual bluegrass

Life cycle: Annual
Origin: Europe
Range: Throughout much of North
   America

Flower color: White
Height: 4–12 inches (10–30.5 cm)

Barnyardgrass

Echinochloa crus-galli

Watergrass, panic grass, cockspur grass, cocksfoot panicum, barngrass

Site, soil, and season: This summer annual sprouts in spring and dies back after hard frost. More seedlings appear following summer rains. It is often seen in ditches and low, damp spots yet likes the rich, moist soil of gardens and irrigated farmland, too. Barnyardgrass is seriously weakened by shade.

Description: Although barnyardgrass can grow 1 to 4 feet tall, the plants first appear as slender upright seedlings. They may show some maroon on the main stems, which become flat rather than round as the plants age and begin to bunch. The leaves are light green (especially compared to crabgrasses) and rarely show any hairs at all along the edges. Barnyardgrass leaves are about ½ inch wide with a folded crease down the middle. Several branches usually grow from a central crown.

Barnyardgrass plants develop seed branches that may stick out diagonally from the central crown or be quite erect. Leaves grow alternately (rather than opposite one another) at widely spaced intervals along these round seed branches. The seedheads are usually composed of a central spike with several short lateral spikes attached to it. The tip and each of these arms are studded with tiny green beadlike seeds. The tip of each seed is also topped with a hairy bristle, though the length of the bristle varies from ½ inch long to only ⅛ inch long, depending on the strain or subspecies. Sometimes these bristles are purplish in color, but they may be green. On small plants the entire seed branch is only a few inches long, while in larger plants it can be more than a foot long.

Healthy, well-fed barnyardgrass plants can continue to produce seeds for a long time — over a million seeds in the course of a summer. But that's only one of the reasons why this weed has been so successful. It uses nitrogen from other crops, and when uncontrolled in a vegetable garden, barnyardgrass can cut production in half. The seeds can remain viable in the soil for 15 years or more.

Control: Pull out young plants when you spot them. The shallow roots are easy to pull, especially when the soil is wet. Adolescent plants may be hoed into submission, but make sure the roots are not left partially buried in damp soil, for they will take root and the plant will start growing again.

Barnyardgrass often grows near gardens in ditches and waste places, which results in a steady "rain" of unwanted seeds into the garden. Mow these areas in mid and late summer before the barnyardgrass (and other weeds) develop mature seeds. Determined foragers may want to sample barnyardgrass seeds baked into bread or used as a crunchy topping on muffins. ■

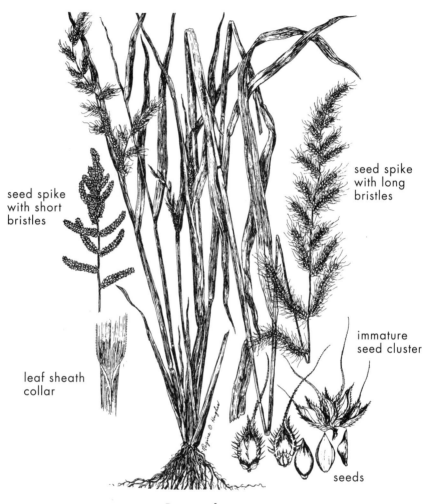

seed spike with short bristles

seed spike with long bristles

leaf sheath collar

immature seed cluster

seeds

Barnyardgrass

Life cycle: Annual
Origin: India and Europe
Range: Throughout the United States, especially in warmer areas and

maritime climates; very common in western and central states
Flower color: Purple or green (bristles)
Height: 1–4 feet (30–122 cm)

Bermudagrass

Cynodon dactylon

Wiregrass, scutch grass, dogs-tooth-grass, devil grass

Site, soil and season: Bermudagrass does not grow well in deep shade but otherwise knows no habitat boundaries. It becomes dormant when temperatures are consistently below 55°F and begins growing when temperatures rise above that point. In summer this grass grows very fast, and a single sprig can increase to cover a square yard in only a few weeks' time. Flower and seed production season stretches from mid-summer to fall.

Description: Most of the bermudagrass encountered as weeds in gardens are descendants of a cultivar called Coastal that was widely planted in the Southeast early in this century (it's a great pasture grass, descended from both the African and Indian strains). Yet many different strains of wild bermudagrass exist that vary greatly in size. They all have the same aggressive growth habit.

Bermudagrass has thin blades, creased down the center. The blades grow from little stems attached to larger, flattish creeping stems. These creeping stems develop roots at almost every node that touches damp soil (nodes are the places where leaves and stems join together, or, in the case of bermudagrass, where the main creeping stems and second-ary stems join together). In warm weather these creeping stems grow very fast, and may easily grow to 2 or 3 feet long, occasionally branch-ing along the way. They love to take secret journeys into vegetable and flower beds, where they can hide under taller plants.

Bermudagrass is aggressive below ground, too. Cream-colored roots form tangled knots below established plants and quickly spread in all directions. New plants develop on buds that grow from these roots. Bermudagrass roots and stems are very tough and stringy and deserve the nickname of wiregrass.

Although bermudagrass does develop seeds on finger-branched flower spikes (they look like miniature versions of crabgrass spikes), it spreads primarily from bits of root and stem left behind after weeding or cultivation or from plant pieces imported in soil or nursery stock. Seed production is much higher in the South than in the North.

In addition to its invasiveness, bermudagrass releases chemicals into the soil which hinder the growth of other plants.

Control: Getting rid of established bermudagrass is very difficult. I have gardened with it (or in spite of it) for nearly 20 years and now employ a number of methods to keep it at bay. Here are 5 of them:

- **Dig it.** I use a spade to dig out every plant I can find, including all roots, every fall and every spring. Dig when the weather is nice — this is very hard work!
- **Put winter to work.** Leave cultivated soil unmulched through several hard freezes. Hard freezes do not normally kill bermudagrass, but when the grass is chopped into little pieces, cold weather does take a certain toll.
- **Mulch heavily.** Bermudagrass can run both above and below mulches, but the presence of a mulch makes it possible to pull — rather than dig — to get rid of this invader.
- **Edge beds.** Bermudagrass has no respect for flexible plastic edging, but it is slowed down by boards, 6-inch wide paving stones, and thick deposits of mulch. (It will run under bricks, concrete blocks, and other stone barriers.) Surprisingly, the edging/ground cover plant known as liriope makes a good barrier plant for keeping bermuda out of flowerbeds.
- **Solarize it.** When I want to make a new garden bed in a spot that is thick with bermuda, I dig out what I can and then cover the space with clear plastic for three to five weeks in summer. This helps weaken remaining plant pieces. A fall-to-winter cover crop gets the soil in condition for gardening and further discourages the bermuda. It's tempting to give up the bermudagrass fight and reach for a herbicide, but that won't solve the problem, either. Researchers have found that herbicides can give one season's relief from bermudagrass, but it will be back the next year. Gardeners who edge their beds with herbicides in spring find that the bermudagrass outgrows the chemical border after about six weeks.

Cultivated counterparts: Most of the bermudagrass sold as sod for lawns is better behaved than wild bermuda, but it still can be invasive. Turf-quality bermuda can only be purchased as sod; it has been bred to grow short, compact stems, and most strains do not produce seeds. Improved bermuda lawns grow best when they are mowed often and fertilized regularly. Like wild bermuda, it does not grow well in shade. ■

Bermudagrass

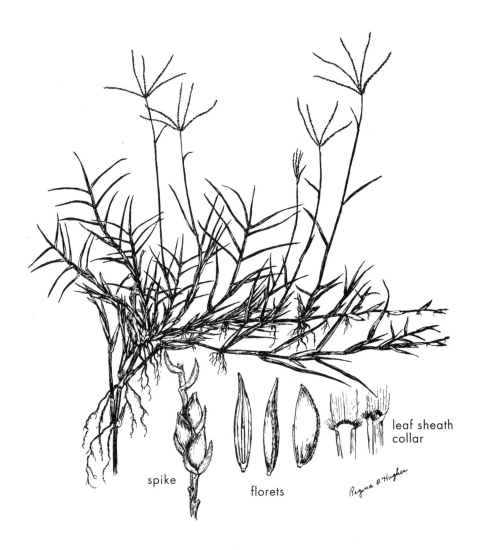

spike

florets

Regina O. Hughes

leaf sheath
collar

Bermudagrass

Life cycle: Perennial

Origin: India and Africa

Range: 20 million acres across the South; central Washington, Colorado,

Connecticut, and New York

Flower color: Green

Height: 6–18 inches (15–46 cm)

Hairy crabgrass

Digitaria sanguinalis

Crabgrass, crowfoot grass, finger grass, pigeon grass, polish millet

Smooth crabgrass

Digitaria ischaemum

Crabgrass, crowfoot grass, finger grass, pigeon grass, polish millet

Goosegrass

Eleusine indica

Crabgrass, crowfoot grass, finger grass, pigeon grass, polish millet, silver crabgrass

Site, soil, and season: Crabgrasses are annuals that grow from seed that sprouts in spring and summer, following rain or irrigation. Most goosegrass plants grow as annuals, too, but in mild winter areas they can survive for a second year. Both crabgrass and goosegrass colonize many different types of soil and are found in gardens, perennial flowerbeds, lawns, and along roadsides. Any time soil is disturbed, crabgrass quickly finds it. It is among the fastest growing of all weeds.

Description: Crabgrass and goosegrass look very much alike, especially as young seedlings. Until the plants develop several stems, it is nearly impossible to tell them apart.

Both goosegrass and crabgrass stems spiral out from a central crown and tend to lie flat, close to the ground. When these stems are a few inches long, differences between the species become evident. The base of the stems on goosegrass is noticeably flattened and usually light green or nearly white. In comparison, the basal portions of crabgrass stems are rounded and more likely to show purplish coloring than white.

The hairs on the 2 grasses are slightly different, too. If you look at a goosegrass plant with a magnifying glass under very bright light, you will see a number of glistening hairs that stick out at wild angles from the places where new leaves emerge from the folded leaf sheaths. These streaming gossamer hairs also emerge from leaf edges on the lowest half-inch of the leaves.

Crabgrass stems and leaves have hairs as well, but they are more uniform and almost downy. Longish hairs adorn the collars of the leaf sheaths but not the leaf edges. Smooth crabgrass is less hairy than hairy crabgrass.

As plants become older, crabgrass stems often develop small roots along the low stems that touch the ground, whereas goosegrass stems do not. If allowed to grow, goosegrass stems stay close to the ground and rarely grow taller than 2 feet, while crabgrass may stand more than 2 feet tall when it grows in rich, moist soil.

The "flowers" of both grasses consist of 3 to 12 short spikes attached to a central stem like the fingers of a hand. On crabgrass the "fingers" hold only small pebbly seed capsules, but goosegrass "fingers" show a heavy black beard. Abundant speck-sized seeds of all species travel from place to place by air, water, bird droppings, and the soles of your shoes.

Control: Mowing seems to encourage these grasses since they can lie close to the ground and escape serious injury. In early summer, you can tell if either of these grasses has invaded your lawn since both grow faster than lawn grasses. To keep a small lawn problem from becoming a big one, pull out the plants when the soil is wet and never allow crabgrass or goosegrass to shed seed in your yard.

Both of these grasses are very serious weeds in vegetable and flower gardens. As long as their roots are securely tucked into soil they can tolerate hot, dry conditions, but when hoed loose from the soil they quickly dry up and die. Hoe out the plants you can, and hand weed close to small flowers and vegetables. Then, as soon as the soil is weeded, water it well and cover with a mulch. Germination of both of these grasses is sparse at best beneath a light-blocking mulch.

Established goosegrass has a very strong root system that is difficult to pull out by hand. Dig under the clump with a turning fork or spade and then pull up the plant. ■

Crabgrass seeds begin germinating in spring, but goosegrass waits for steady warmth. The first goosegrass seedlings normally appear about six weeks after crabgrass starts grabbing garden space.

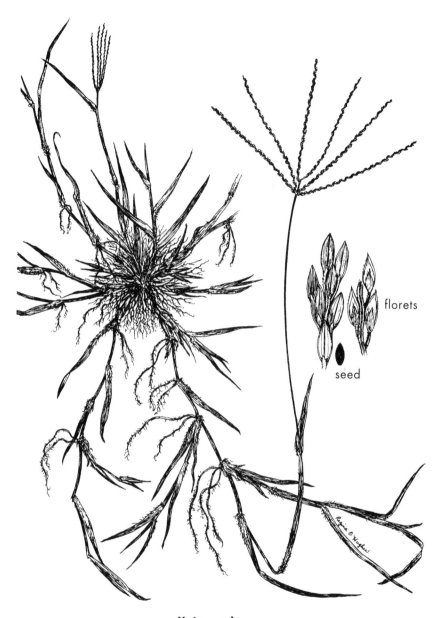

florets

seed

Hairy crabgrass

Life cycle: Annual
Origin: Europe
Range: All over the world; very common
  in the North and South

Flower color: Green
Height: 1–3 feet (30–91 cm)

Crabgrasses

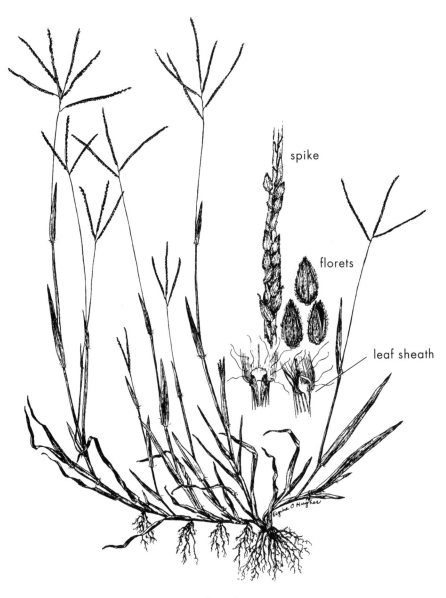

spike

florets

leaf sheath

Smooth crabgrass

Life cycle: Annual

Origin: Europe

Range: All over the world; very common in the North and South

Flower color: Green

Height: 1–2 feet (30–61 cm)

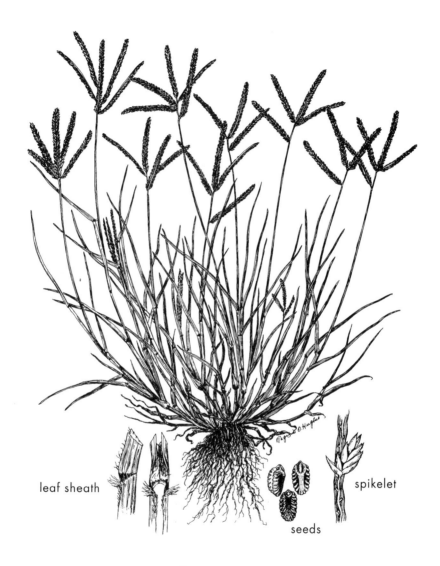

leaf sheath

seeds

spikelet

Goosegrass

Life cycle: Annual

Origin: Asia

Range: All over the world; most common in the central and southern states

Flower color: Black beard

Height: 6–18 inches (15–46 cm)

Crabgrasses

Giant foxtail

Setaria faberi

Giant bristle grass, nodding foxtail

Green foxtail

Setaria viridis

Bottle grass, green bristle grass, wild millet

Yellow foxtail

Setaria glauca

Pale pigeon grass, yellow bristle grass

Site, soil and season: The foxtails are summer annuals that sprout from early spring to midsummer and show seedheads from midsummer to frost. They grow in all types of soil, in sun or partial shade, and may grow as individuals or in groups. The roots of foxtails are quite skimpy, so they easily survive in thin, shallow soils that are heavy with rocks.

Description: These annual grasses are quite familiar to gardeners, though it can be difficult to tell exactly which type of foxtail you have. The 3 species develop very similar-looking seedheads studded with numerous small hairs, so that they look like little foxes' tails. The "tails" of green and yellow foxtail are usually 2 to 4 inches long and always straight. Giant foxtail's tail may be as long as 6 inches, but it is slightly curved. All foxtails bear small oval-shaped seeds, which may be yellowish or dark brown.

You can often distinguish the different foxtails according to their height and hairiness. Green foxtail is smaller than the others, with a maximum height of 2 feet, and its leaves are hairless. Yellow foxtail can grow to 3 feet or more, and the base of each leaf (where it emerges from the stem) has numerous long hairs on the inside curve. Giant foxtail often grows 5 to 7 feet tall and falls over. Little hairs are scattered all over the leaves of giant foxtail.

All of the foxtails are bothersome weeds in gardens. If allowed to grow uncontrolled, they can shade out smaller seedlings and hinder the growth of larger plants, too. Canadian scientists found that green foxtail reduced potato yields by more than 20 percent if the foxtail was not removed during the first two weeks after the potatoes broke ground. Allowing the foxtail to stay for a full 10 weeks cut potato production by a whopping 75 percent!

Control: If foxtail is a chronic unwanted visitor in your garden, do everything you can to avoid introducing new seeds. Pull out plants as soon as you

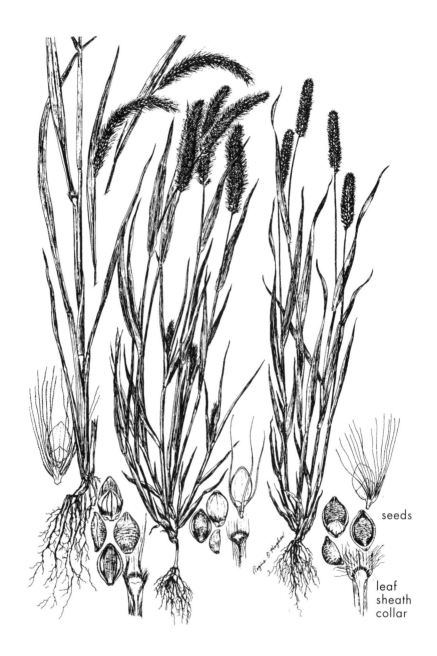

seeds

leaf
sheath
collar

Giant foxtail   Green foxtail   Yellow foxtail

Life cycle: Summer annuals

Origin: Europe

Range: Throughout much of North America

Flower color: Green or yellow-green

Height: Giant, 5–7 feet (152–213 cm); Green, 1–2 feet (30–61 cm); Yellow, 2–3 feet (61–91 cm)

Foxtails

see them, preferably when the soil is wet. In your vegetable garden, use mulches and cover crops to stop germination of foxtail seeds. In lawns, mow down plants before they can develop seeds.

You can accidentally make foxtail deposits in your soil's weed seed bank by bringing in manure that contains foxtail seeds. Foxtail seeds easily survive the digestive tracts of stock animals, and seeds buried in soil can remain viable for 5 years or more.

As long as foxtail plants do not hold mature seeds, it's fine to toss them into your compost heap. Young green seedheads make interesting additions to cut flower arrangements. ∎

What's in a Name?

The genus name *Setaria* comes from the Latin word *seta*, which means bristle. So, bristle grass is a more accurate (if less poetic) common name for the foxtails.

Johnsongrass
Sorghum halepense

Egyptian grass, Morocco millet, false guinea grass

Site, soil, and season: This large perennial clump-forming grass grows best in fertile lowland fields but can tolerate many different types of soil if it gets full sun. It is considered noxious. It was introduced as a forage grass and quickly established itself in farm fields of the South and gradually spread northward.

Description: Johnsongrass sprouts in early spring from thick underground rhizomes, or creeping roots. It usually appears as a slender clump of upright stems with straplike leaves. The central vein that runs the length of the leaf is white, fading to green near the leaf tips.

If you dig up the plant, you will find a thick pinkish root attached to the clump at a right angle. The roots are covered with large sheaths, or scales. If the plant is one of many in a colony, these roots will spread all through the soil. They are brittle and break into pieces when disturbed.

Johnsongrass also grows readily from seed. The seedlings look somewhat like very dark green corn seedlings and usually have a dark purple main stem. Seedlings usually do not produce underground rhizomes until quite late in their first summer.

When plants are 2 to 4 feet tall, they develop large spreading panicles of florets composed of many small branches that grow opposite one another from the slender floret stalk. Purplish sheaths loosely cover the flowers, which adorn the entire panicle, often with short, angled hairs emerging from the ends of the florets. New seed-bearing panicles continue to develop until frost. The plants die back to their roots after hard freezes.

Control: As your first step toward stopping the spread of this aggressive grass, dig out as much as you can of the clump and its roots. When digging a large clump, try to lift it from the ground intact and drop it into a cart or wheelbarrow, soil and all. Knock the soil from the roots and spread the plants and roots out in the sun where they can dry. Sift through the soil left behind and pick out bits of broken root. Dispose of dried johnsongrass plants in a dry heap. Compost them after several months have passed and all plant parts are thoroughly dead.

Since the root rhizomes break off easily, it's very difficult to eradicate every last piece in a single digging. Go back after a month or so and dig again to remove new sprouts.

Johnsongrass roots can be killed by freezing temperatures below 25°F. However, when buried in the soil more than a few inches deep, they have no trouble surviving winter air temperatures below 0°F. Smaller root pieces are more likely to freeze to death than large ones, so cultivating in late fall, and again in the middle of winter, can help to weaken and kill root pieces left behind in the soil.

Sometimes johnsongrass establishes itself in perennial plantings, such as asparagus and strawberry beds. If the infestation is severe, you will need to take up your crop plants (while they are dormant) and move them to a new location. When you've removed as much johnsongrass as you can find, grow a cover crop or a thick stand of beans to suppress any johnsongrass that tries to resprout.

Mow down johnsongrass growing along roadsides near your garden to keep its seeds from invading your cultivated spaces. Regular mowing also weakens the rootstocks and brings them closer to the surface, where they are more likely to be killed by severe cold or drought. ∎

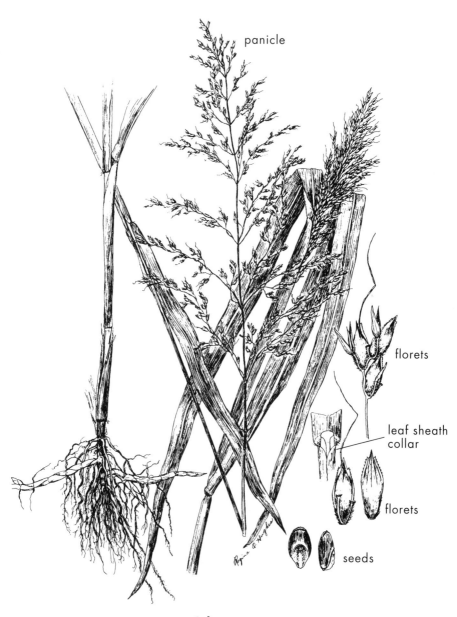

panicle

florets

leaf sheath
collar

florets

seeds

Johnsongrass

Life cycle: Perennial
Origin: Southern Europe and Asia
Range: Florida to southwestern Ontario
and westward in elevations below

4,000 feet
Flower color: Greenish tan with purple
sheath
Height: 2–6 feet (61–183 cm)

Yellow nutsedge
Cyperus esculentus

Nutgrass, chufa, coco sedge, rush nut, edible galingale, earth almond

Site, soil and season: Yellow nutsedge grows best in damp, compacted places, but it can make itself at home in a wide range of situations. New plants emerge by early summer and may or may not develop flower spikes by early fall.

Description: Yellow nutsedge is a very slender, upright grasslike plant that shows no tendencies to spread outward — at least from the above-ground point of view. Individual leaves are up to ½ inch across and may grow 1 to 2 feet long. In dry weather, the outer leaves turn brown, and only the inside ones remain light green.

Where you see one nutsedge plant, you usually see many more, for this weed usually grows from small nutlike corms that are produced on the roots. If you dig or pull up a plant, several of the roots will be cream-colored and covered with scaly structures and may be several inches longer than the other roots. These are the roots that produce the nuts.

Nutsedge can grow from seeds, too. The seed-producing part of the plant is a slender stem that grows from the plant's center. A loose cluster of yellowish flowering spikes bursts from the top of this stem and eventually develops numerous ⅛-inch-long yellow-brown seeds.

Plants may develop the subterranean nuts (which look like tiny footballs) or flower spikes, or may reproduce themselves both ways. The nuts are edible. Native Americans ate them raw or roasted — when raw they taste like coconut, and roasted they resemble almonds. The official name of this edible part is chufa.

But please, do not allow nutsedge to take over your garden so you can munch a bunch of chufas. Farmers have long known that nutsedge caused corn and other crops to suffer, and the scientific explanation is that nutsedge hosts and encourages soil-dwelling bacteria that destroy nitrogen that would otherwise be used by plants.

Control: Persistence is required to get rid of yellow nutsedge, for the corms can persist in soil for several seasons. Plants can be pulled up easily when they are growing in soft, moist soil, or in sites that are covered with mulch. Yet you never know if you've gotten every nut when you pull plants up, for the nuts tend to break off. You will seldom see them attached to nice healthy roots; as soon as the nut is ready, the mother plant cuts it loose.

Thoroughly dig out nutsedge plants in fall. In addition, this weed may be discouraged by improving the drainage in the spot where it grows. Where digging and bed renovation are impractical, mulch heavily and pull up plants as soon as you see them. In this way you can eliminate yellow nutsedge in a couple of seasons. ■

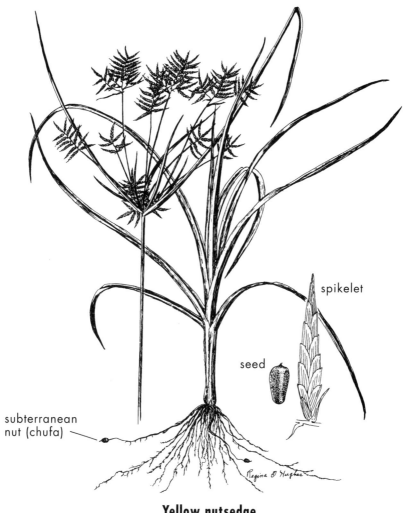

spikelet

seed

subterranean nut (chufa)

Yellow nutsedge

Life cycle: Perennial
Origin: Native
Range: Throughout the United States and southern Canada; but most common in the eastern and southeastern part of this range
Flower color: Yellow
Height: 1–3 feet (30–91 cm)

Quackgrass

Agropyron repens

Couchgrass, quitchgrass, creeping wheat

Site, soil, and season: Although perennial, quackgrass is considered a cool-season plant that grows best when temperatures are mild. The tops die back in winter, though the roots continue to develop buds until the ground freezes. New plants emerge from early spring until midsummer, with a final flush of new growth in the fall. Quackgrass grows in all types of garden situations except deep shade. It is also a common pasture grass and roadside weed.

Description: Quackgrass is a rough-looking perennial grass that usually grows to between 1 and 3 feet tall. Established plants look like clumps, but if an infested place has been dug or tilled, the plants are smaller and look more like a mat. If you dig them up, you will find that the small plants are attached to one another through a vast network of underground creeping stems. Roots emerge from these straw-colored underground stems at obvious joints. Some joints give rise to new plants that push to the surface on smooth stems. The entire mess shatters like glass when handled.

Above the ground, quackgrass leaves emerge from slender stems alternately (rather than opposite one another), and there are little joints every few inches along the stems. Generally raggedy in appearance, quackgrass often turns partially brown during hot spells in midsummer.

Mowed plants may not develop seeds, but most quackgrass plants send up small spikes that look like skinny wheat tops. However, quackgrass's primary means of spreading is by stretching out its underground rhizomes, which release chemicals into the soil that inhibit the growth of other plants.

Control: Quackgrass must be very carefully dug out, for if you chop the roots to bits, each little piece is capable of growing into a new plant. So, locate the most robust crown in a colony and begin your digging by loosening the soil around it with a digging fork. Now go after the quackgrass with your fingers, gently lifting each tuft from the loose soil with roots attached. Many of the smaller plants will still be attached to larger ones, and you'll likely feel like you're digging up a spider web of roots. Pick up all the little pieces of root that break off as you work. Finally pull out the largest plants, and if you can, leave the spot alone for a couple of weeks. Then go back and dig through again, removing

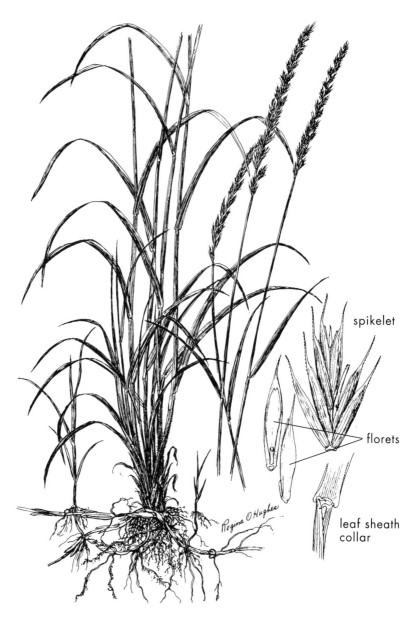

spikelet

florets

leaf sheath
collar

Regina O'Hughes

Quackgrass

Life cycle: Perennial
Origin: Eurasia
Range: Northern half of the United States and in southern Canada; occasionally in warmer climates
Flower color: Green to tan
Height: 1–3 feet (30–91 cm)

bits of root that were left behind. If you've done your job well, the spot is now ready to be planted with something you want to grow. A second digging in fall is usually needed to eradicate quackgrass totally.

After you finish a digging session, rinse off the tools you have used to keep from spreading the root pieces to new locations. Avoid rototilling space infested with quackgrass, or you may spread it out of control.

Thoroughly dry quackgrass plants in the sun before attempting to compost them. Or dump them in damp shade and let them rot there.

Complete eradication of an established colony of quackgrass may require two seasons of effort, but it can be done. In large infested areas, fall tillage that exposes mangled roots to harsh winter weather can be very helpful. Grow your crop plants close together or use smother crops to further stress resident quackgrass. ■

Does your mulch go quack?

Hay mulch is great stuff, but if you live where quackgrass is extremely common, be a picky mulch shopper. Quackgrass seeds travel easily in hay and survive the digestive tracts of animals who eat it. Since quackgrass is allowed to grow in many pastures, you can easily bring the seeds into your garden in innocent-looking hay and manure.

We'd love your thoughts...

Your reactions, criticisms, things you did or didn't like about this Storey Book. Please use space below (or write a letter if you'd prefer — even send photos!) telling how you've made use of the information . . . how you've put it to work . . . the more details the better! Thanks in advance for your help in building our library of good Storey Books.

Pamela B. Art

Publisher

Book Title: _____

Purchased From: _____

Comments: _____

_____

_____

_____

_____

_____

_____

Your Name: _____

Address: _____

☐ Please check here if you'd like our latest Storey's Books for Country Living Catalog.

☐ You have my permission to quote from my comments, and use these quotations in ads, brochures, mail, and other promotions used to market your books.

Signed _____ Date _____

email=Feedback@Storey.Com

PRINTED IN USA   10/95

From: _____

BUSINESS REPLY MAIL

FIRST CLASS MAIL   PERMIT NO. 2   POWNAL, VT

POSTAGE WILL BE PAID BY ADDRESSEE

STOREY'S BOOKS FOR COUNTRY LIVING
STOREY COMMUNICATIONS, INC.
105 SCHOOLHOUSE ROAD
POWNAL VT 05261-9988

CHAPTER 5

A GALLERY
OF
VINING WEEDS

WEEDS THAT GROW as vines pose special problems, for their growth habit makes it possible for them to invade the garden virtually unnoticed. Then you suddenly realize that your clematis arbor has turned into morningglory or that your sweet potatoes have become bindweeds. Get to know all of the vining weeds that turn up in your garden so you can eliminate them when they're young, before they get a stranglehold on your favorite plants.

If you miss a few and discover them after they've tied themselves in knots around your plants (but before they've begin to flower) you do not need to untangle the stems and pull them out unless you really want to do so. Instead, sever the base of the vine with pruning shears and let it die still bound around other plants. Pulling out an extensive vine may mangle its support plant so badly that it's not worth doing.

Field bindweed

Convolvulus arvensis

Woodbine, pear bine, lady's nightcap, wild morningglory, creeping jenny, hedge bells, possession vine

Hedge bindweed

Convolvulus sepium

Woodbine, pear bine, lady's nightcap, wild morningglory, creeping jenny, hedge bells, possession vine

Site, soil, and season: The bindweeds thrive in full sun and occur in vegetable and flower gardens as well as ditches and other waste places. True herbaceous perennials, they disappear in winter and sprout from underground roots first thing in spring. Flowering begins in late spring in the South and in midsummer in northern areas and continues until frost.

First seen in Virginia in 1739, field bindweed is firmly established as one of the nastiest weeds in northern North America and is now classified in the world's top 10 worst weeds. The Midwest became infested in the late 1800s when immigrants accidentally imported the seeds with wheat seed. It spread to the Pacific Northwest when a farmer used it to cover crop his orchard. By 1922, field bindweed was listed as California's worst weed. All this time, bindweed's spread was helped along by gardeners who planted it as an ornamental, mostly in hanging baskets. Hedge bindweed is more often seen in ditches and waste places than in gardens.

Description: The differences between field bindweed and hedge bindweed relate to size, with hedge bindweed having larger leaves and flowers. The leaves of both species are dark green, shaped like elongated arrowheads, and grow alternately from twining stems. If the vines can find no upright plants to support them, they grow into a tangled ground cover.

Flowers of field bindweed are about 1 inch across when open, and may be pink, white, or pink and white. Hedge bindweed flowers are larger, often 2 inches across, and pure white or white with a pinkish cast. Flowers of both species look like morningglories, for that's exactly what they are.

Both bindweeds grow from spreading underground roots. Field bindweed's roots may reach 30 feet below ground, which accounts for its seeming indestructibility in the garden. Hedge bindweed's roots are not so deep and extensive but still can regenerate new topgrowth many times over.

The bindweeds can be confused with wild buckwheat, which has a similar growth habit but does not have morningglory-like flowers or tenacious perennial roots. (See page 176 for more information on wild buckwheat.)

Control: If you have a small colony of either type of bindweed, the best cure is to dig out the roots as soon as the plants show themselves. This can be difficult, as the roots break to pieces at a slight touch. They are less brittle following heavy rains. Use a digging fork rather than a spade to keep from slicing the roots into little pieces. With field bindweed, root pieces only ½ inch long can sprout into new plants.

Digging out bindweed can be challenging, since you'd expect to find the roots spread out in a logical pattern, such as in a circle around the place where the vine emerges from the soil. Bindweed ensures its survival by having roots that change directions in wacky ways. Most of the turns, or elbows, in a bindweed root have buds, which can easily grow into new plants. Dig until you think you've got it all and then dig some more. Use a heavy mulch over places where bindweed has been, for some root pieces survive the most diligent digging. Cardboard covered with leaves or another organic mulch is excellent.

Where a thick stand of bindweed is well established, plan a two-year assault. The first year, let the bindweed grow until early summer and then mow it down before it flowers. At that point, it has been living on food reserves stored in the roots for several weeks, and when you lop off the topgrowth, you rob the plant of energy. Just don't think you have killed it! In only a week or so, a flush of new plants will push up where there formerly seemed to be but one. Let these little plants grow for 2 or 3 weeks and then mow them down.

Now start digging. If you're dealing with hedge bindweed, you may be able to eradicate it by pulling up all the roots you find in the top foot of soil. Field bindweed is more persistent, and you may encounter new plants the following spring. Dig these out as soon as you see them and mulch heavily to make the digging easier.

Never, ever, allow either type of bindweed to flower in or near your garden, for the seeds remain viable for many years. In one study, 8 percent of 50-year-old bindweed seeds were able to germinate. ■

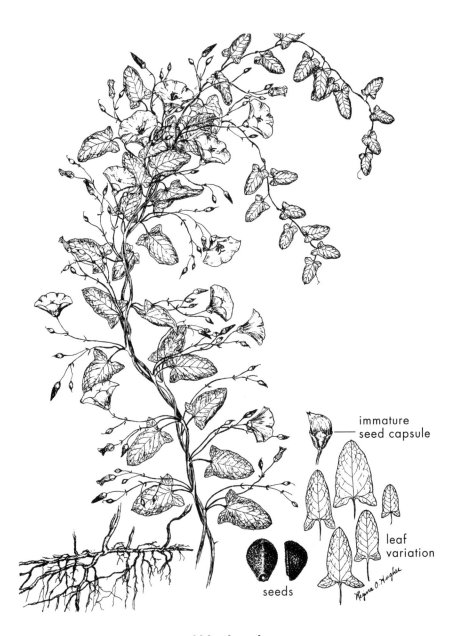

immature
seed capsule

leaf
variation

seeds

Field bindweed

Life cycle: Perennial
Origin: Europe and Asia
Range: Most of North America except
Florida and the arctic regions

Flower color: Pink, white, or pink and
white
Height: 2–7 feet (61–213 cm)

flower

seeds

Hedge bindweed

Life cycle: Perennial
Origin: Eurasia
Range: Eastern two-thirds of North America and Pacific Northwest

Flower color: White or white with a pinkish cast
Height: 3–10 feet (91 cm–3 m)

Wild buckwheat
Polygonum convolvulus

Cornbind, black bindweed, bearbind, ivy bindweed

Site, soil, and season: A summer annual, wild buckwheat is abundant in fields where corn, wheat, or other grains are grown, and in irrigated gardens. It adapts to many different soil types and prefers full sun or partial shade.

Description: This weed is easily confused with field bindweed (see page 172), but there are several ways to tell the difference between the two species. Wild buckwheat is an annual twining vine that also creeps along the ground. The leaves are heart-shaped, 1 to 3 inches long and broader at the shoulders than those of bindweed. Wild buckwheat leaves have smooth edges and very pointed tips. The plants usually branch into 2 or 3 vining stems near the base, and the main stems develop additional branches as the plants grow. Vines grow 1 to 3 feet long and wind around the stems of taller plants in a counterclockwise direction. If they do not find taller plants to lean on, the stems lie on the ground and wind around each other. Roots are fibrous, with no tubers or rhizomes.

Small clusters of greenish-white flowers develop on slender spikes, which grow from the place where leaves join the main stem. The flowers look nothing like the morningglory-type blooms of field bindweeds and are so small that you must search to see them. Wild buckwheat seeds are black, triangular, and can be extremely abundant in the soil.

Control: Pull up plants as soon as you are able to recognize the heart-shaped leaves. Wild buckwheat also can be hoed into submission, for the plants do not grow back from bits of root left behind in the soil. ∎

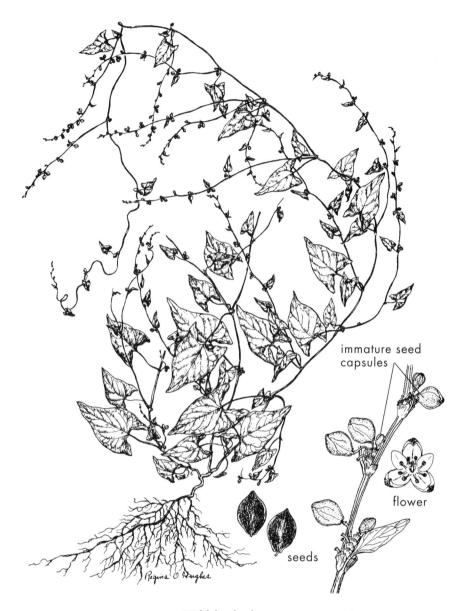

immature seed capsules

flower

seeds

Wild buckwheat

Life cycle: Annual	**Flower color:** Greenish-white
Origin: Asia, via Europe	**Height:** 1–3 feet (30–91 cm)
Range: Throughout the United States and southern Canada	

Dodder

Cuscuta species

Devil's hair, goldthread vine, hairweed

Site, soil, and season: Dodder can occur anywhere and has been known to travel in the root balls of nursery and bedding plants. Since dodder plants live on other plants, they show little preference for soil types, though some species are best adapted to low, wet places. Most dodder seedlings emerge in midspring, but more germinate throughout the growing season. *C. indecora,* also known as Chilean or largeseed dodder, has the largest range of host plants.

Description: The most bizarre member of the morningglory family, dodder is a true parasitic plant. Unable to manufacture chlorophyll of its own, dodder "robs" other plants of theirs by twining around the host plant and sending rootlike projections into its host's stem. Dodder looks like a mass of tangled string that rather suddenly appears. The strings (actually dodder stems) are usually yellow or orange, depending on the species, with no true leaves — only sparse scaly projections along the stem.

Dodder plants first appear as slender yellow threads that emerge from the soil and wave about. By the time they are 4 inches high, those that can attach themselves to host plants do and immediately begin twining. Seedlings that do not find hosts die. Once they get going, dodder stems can grow 3 inches per day.

Dodders produce prolific flowers and seeds. The tiny white bell-shaped flowers are borne in clusters, and each flower can produce 4 seeds. By the time dodder plants flower, they have usually fed so heavily on their host plant that it is noticeably stunted.

Control: Pull up host plants afflicted with dodder and destroy them. If the dodder is already blooming, consider burning the entire mass. In fields and meadows, frequent summer mowing can keep a small dodder outbreak from becoming a larger problem. Dodder usually does not persist in places that are cultivated frequently, such as vegetable gardens, but can become a challenge in beds that are seldom disturbed, such as those planted with herbs or shrubs. When you first see dodder on a plant, pull it off and place the dodder in the sun to dry. Go back weekly and remove any additional dodder stems that appear on the plant. ∎

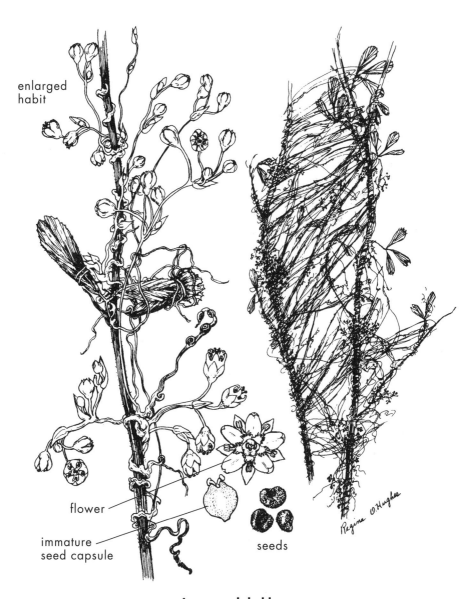

enlarged
habit

flower

immature
seed capsule

seeds

Regina O. Hughes

Largeseed dodder

Life cycle: Annual
Origin: Native and introduced species
Range: Throughout most of North
America

Flower color: White
Height: 3–4 feet (91–122 cm)

Greenbrier
Smilax hispida, Smilax rotundifolia
Catbrier, bullbrier, horse brier, wild sarsaparilla

Site, soil, and season: Prickly greenbrier vines grow wild in eastern woodlands and often find shaded woodland gardens to their liking as well.
They are especially troublesome when they become established among
shade-loving shrubs such as azaleas, or when they wind their way
through the thick foliage of boxwoods. In most species, the stems stay
green through the winter.

Description: This is the same vine that grows in thickets in open woodlands,
making hiking so hazardous that you must seek an alternate route. In
shady gardens, greenbrier is a formidable pest because the vines are so
well armed with slender thorns.

The exact form of the plant varies with species, but the most common
one develops glossy green leaves, sometimes mottled with light green,
that are oval or heart-shaped and have pointed ends. New leaves are
glossy yellow-green. The leaves grow alternately along the stem at
approximately 2-inch intervals. At each place where a leaf joins the
stem, so do 2 curly tendrils about 2 inches long, which tie themselves
around the stems and leaves of other plants.

Thorns are most numerous along the section of stem that is closest to
the ground, but in some species thorns are present all the way to the
tips of the vines. The thorns may be green, reddish, or black, and often
angle upward or downward like little barbs. In late summer, greenbrier
vines develop small flower clusters followed by blue-black berries.

Greenbrier plants may start life as seedlings, but most often sprout
from wandering roots. The roots of some species become quite thick and
have been used to flavor drinks when cleaned and boiled in syrup.
Young leaves also are edible.

Control: Ideally you should dig out plants that invade your garden space, but
this is seldom practical where large shrubs are established — the
preferred habitat for this prickly weed. Instead, cut off the vines with
sharp shears just below the soil's surface and remove them with gloved
hands. The roots left behind in the soil will likely produce new sprouts,
so you will need to repeatedly clean away vines for at least two seasons
to permanently rid the site of greenbrier.

Cultivated Counterparts: A few *Smilax* species that do not have thorns are
grown as ornamentals. In the South, the Jackson vine often grown on

porch railings is a tropical relative of prickly greenbrier. However, the plant known as smilax to florists is not a close cousin but rather is a relative of asparagus. ■

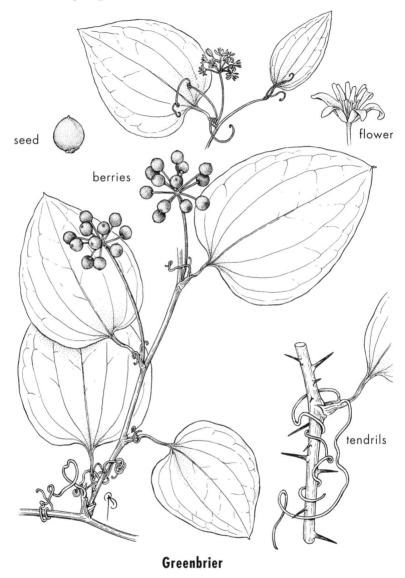

seed

flower

berries

tendrils

Greenbrier

Life cycle: Perennial
Origin: North America
Range: Open woodlands from Nova
    Scotia to Florida and westward to

Michigan and Texas
Flower color: Green
Height: 2–6 feet (61–183 cm)

Tall morningglory

Ipomoea purpurea

None

Ivyleaf morningglory

Ipomea hederacea

None

Site, soil, and season: Both of these annual morningglories need warm soil to germinate. They sprout in mid-to-late spring, and new plants continue to appear all summer. Bloom time lasts from early summer to frost. Morningglories grow in a variety of soils, but they do like full sun.

Description: The seedling leaves of both of these morningglory species have an unusual toothlike shape. After the first 2 leaves appear, the second set of leaves is heart-shaped. The third set of leaves (and those beyond) remains heart-shaped in tall morningglory, but becomes 3-lobed in the ivy-leafed version. Both species have numerous downy hairs on stems and leaves and twine themselves around taller plants.

Flowers of both species open during the morning hours and close by noon. They are very pretty, and tall morningglory is often grown as an ornamental. Tall morningglory blossoms may be blue, purple, white, or variegated. On ivyleaf morningglory, flowers are rose pink or purple, with a lighter colored throat.

Seeds are formed inside round green pods. The seeds are large, as long as ¼ inch, and are dark brown to black. Older plants often host powdery mildew.

Control: Despite their pretty flowers, morningglories tie other plants into messy bundles and can shade out less vigorous crops. They are easiest to control when very young by simply hoeing them down. Later, you can pull up the plants and compost them or simply sever them from their roots and let them dry to death.

Where you see one morningglory you are likely to see a thousand, so try to follow up weeding with a mulch. Morningglories thrive on sun and cannot grow without good light. ■

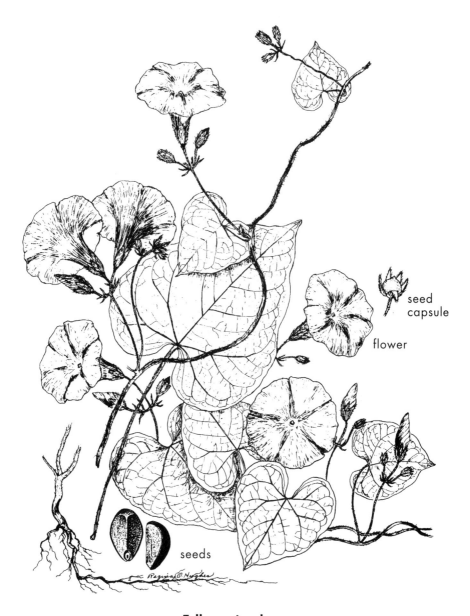

seed
capsule

flower

seeds

Tall morningglory

Life cycle: Annual
Origin: Tropical America
Range: Much of North America, except Rocky Mountains

Flower color: Blue, purple, white, or variegated
Height: 6–10 feet (183 cm–3 m)

Morningglories

Minor Morningglories

Morningglories come in many shapes and sizes, including the 2 weeds described. Here are 3 of the best known ones.

Scarlet Morningglory *I. coccinea*

Annual. Very similar to tall morningglory but has red flowers with long white tubular throats. Found mostly near southeastern coasts.

Cypressvine Morningglory *I. quamoclit*

Annual. Perhaps the best behaved and prettiest of the glories, with very ferny, finely cut leaves and small bright red flowers. Cultivated strains have been developed with other flower colors. If you want to grow a morningglory in your yard, try this one, for it's much less invasive than the others. Still, watch out for an overabundance of volunteers! Seedling leaves very narrow and long.

Bigroot Morningglory *I. pandurata*

Perennial, also known as wild sweet potato. Leaves heart-shaped. Flowers white with purple centers. Heavy yellowish-white roots often found a foot or more below the soil's surface. Found mostly in warm climates, in sandy soils.

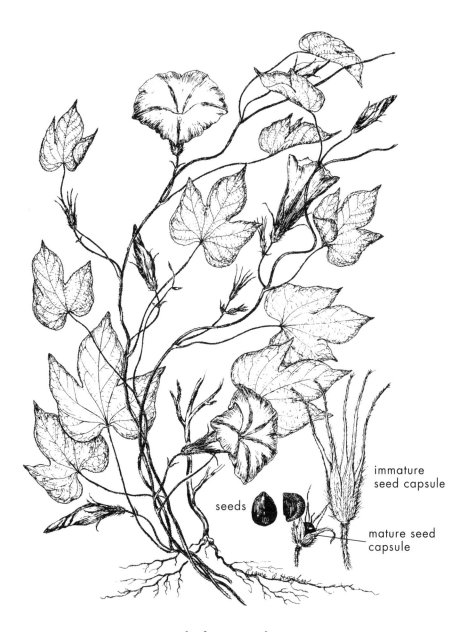

seeds

immature
seed capsule

mature seed
capsule

Ivyleaf morningglory

Life cycle: Annual
Origin: Tropical America
Range: Temperate North America; warm, humid climates

Flower color: Rose pink or purple, with lighter-colored throat
Height: 6–10 feet (183 cm–3 m)

Poison ivy

Poison creeper, mercury

Toxicodendron radicans
(frequently classified as *Rhus radicans*)

Site, soil, and season: A perennial vine with woody roots and stems, poison ivy usually grows as a ground cover until it finds just the right tree (or fence) to climb. It then turns into a persistent vine that clings to its support with strong suckerlike feet, which are actually rootlets. Poison ivy is most at home in shade but often pops up in sunny places, too. Poison ivy is extremely common along the edges of fields and woods, nestled near fences, and is also seen in shady flowerbeds. The leaves die in winter, and new leaves appear in early spring.

Description: The exact appearance of poison ivy varies with the age of the plant and the situation where it grows. All poison ivy has leaves grouped together in threes. These 3 leaves are actually leaflets, each with its own short stem, and each 3-part leaflet emerges alternately (rather than opposite one another) from the main stem.

The first spring leaves are often reddish in color and then quickly change to shiny green. After the leaves turn green, reddish color persists on stems and along the leaf margins of new leaves. Young leaflets often have small notches on their outer edges, while older leaflets are oval in shape, with a pointed tip.

Young plants rarely flower, but old established vines growing on trees often flower by late April or May. The pale green flower clusters are followed by small white berries. These berries persist through winter and are eaten by 55 species of birds. Poison ivy leaves turn red or orange in fall, and the leaves drop as winter begins.

Poison ivy roots, stems, leaves, flowers, and fruits contain a resin called urushiol, which causes severe skin irritation in many people. Other people are immune to its effects, but your immune status can change quite suddenly. Once you become reactive to poison ivy, you must avoid contact with the plant for the rest of your life.

Control: Always wear gloves, long pants, and other protective clothing when dealing with poison ivy. To kill an old vine that has firmly sunk its rootlets into the trunk of a tree, begin by cutting through the plant base with a sharp knife. As long as you're stuck with a knife laced with urushiol, make additional nicks along the main vine to make sure the plant is terminally girdled.

flowers

seeds

aerial
roots

Poison ivy

Life cycle: Perennial
Origin: North America
Range: Throughout woods, yards, and sometimes gardens in the United States and southern Canada, more common in the East than in the West
Flower color: Pale green
Height: 1–20 feet (30 cm–6 m)

When a few poison ivy plants pop up here and there, sever them with long-handled pruning shears and allow them to dry until dead. Never burn poison ivy, for its toxins can be breathed into your lungs in the smoke. Sheep and goats will often eat poison ivy.

I make an exception to my antiherbicide policy for poison ivy because the plant itself is so dangerous. Several widely available products give lasting control of poison ivy, but they must be applied exactly right. I have gotten good results by spot treating individual poison ivy plants with a glyphosate herbicide, but some of the newer herbicides that are applied to leaves should work as well.

Wait for a warm, dry day in late spring or early summer to declare chemical war on your poison ivy. Dilute the chemical according to label directions and apply it to every green poison ivy leaf you see. They should wither and turn brown within a week. To kill poison ivy that had invaded a lovely ground cover, I used a small paintbrush to apply the herbicide to the poison ivy leaves so I could kill them without injuring the surrounding plants. ■

Bad Guys and Good Guys

Memorize this rhyme:

> "Leaves of three, let it be;
> leaves of five, let it thrive."

The "leaves of three" warning applies to poison ivy as well as poison oak, a common woodland plant that grows on a woody stem, much like a one- or two-year-old sapling tree. Poison oak's three leaves are very dark green and glossy, shaped like long pointed ovals that are usually about 6 inches long. The "leaves of five" part of the phrase refers to Virginia creeper, a harmless native vine that often grows in the same places as poison ivy.

◄ CHAPTER 6 ►

WEEDY FAMILY
RELATIONS

IF YOUR WEEDS still have you stumped, maybe learning more about their families will help. In addition to being similar in appearance, plant families tend to share similar soil preferences, pests, and life cycles. Here are brief sketches of 28 plant families, and common weeds and cultivated plants that belong to each of them.

Aizoaceae
In North America this family is mostly made up of weeds and wayside plants, including carpetweed *(Mollugo verticillata)*.

Amaranthaceae
Weedy members of this family include all the pigweeds *(Amaranthus* species) and close relations such as grain amaranth and Oriental amaranths that have been selected for use as cooked greens.

Anacardiaceae
Woodland plants including poison ivy *(Toxicodendron radicans)*, poison oak, and poison sumac make up this family.

Asclepiadaceae
This small group includes butterfly weed and milkweeds such as the common species, *Asclepias syriaca*.

Campanulaceae
Commonly known as the bluebell family, the campanulas include numerous cultivated flowers called bluebells and bellflowers, as well as the invasive weed known as creeping bellflower *(Campanula rapunculoides)*.

Caryophyllaceae

Commonly known as the pink family, this group includes all flowers classified as dianthus, as well as the chickweeds *(Stellaria media, Cerastium vulgatum)* and many less common weeds of fall-sown grains.

Chenopodiaceae

This small group of plants includes lambsquarters *(Chenopodium album)* and some tumbleweeds. They are sometimes called the goosefoot family.

Compositae

The largest plant family on earth, the Composites include most plants with flowers that have petals radiating from a central eye, such as black-eyed susans, zinnias, and sunflowers. Weedy members of this family include:

- Canada thistle, *Cirsium arvense*
- Cocklebur, *Xanthium strumarium*
- Dandelion, *Taraxacum officinale*
- Galinsoga, *Galinsoga ciliata*
- Wild lettuces, *Lactuca* species
- Ragweeds, *Ambrosia* species
- Sowthistles, *Sonchus* species
- Spanishneedles, *Bidens bipinnata*

Convolvulaceae

Commonly called the morningglory family, this clan includes sweet potatoes as well as the following weeds:

- Bindweeds, *Convolvulus* species
- Dodders, *Cuscuta* species
- Morningglories, *Ipomoea* species

Cruciferae

The Crucifers include the cole crops (cabbage, broccoli, cauliflower), as well as turnips, radishes, and these well-known weeds:

- Mustards, *Brassica* species
- Pepperweeds, *Lepidium* species
- Shepherd's purse, *Capsella bursa-pastoris*

Cyperaceae

The sedge family includes yellow nutsedge *(Cyperus esculentus)* and several ornamental grasses.

Euphorbiaceae

A huge group of plants, the euphorbias include many cultivated flowers and all of the weeds known as spurges *(Euphorbia species)*.

Geraniaceae

All of the true geraniums (including the scented ones) are cousins to weedy Carolina geranium *(Geranium carolinianum)*.

Gramineae

The grass family includes corn, wheat, oats, and many other edible grains with strap-like, grassy leaves, along with these weeds:

- Annual bluegrass, *Poa annua*
- Barnyardgrass, *Echinochloa crus-galli*
- Bermudagrass, *Cynodon dactylon*
- Crabgrasses, *Digitaria* species
- Foxtails, *Setaria* species
- Goosegrass, *Eleusine indica*
- Johnsongrass, *Sorghum halepense*
- Quackgrass, *Agropyron repens*

Labiatae

Best known as the mint family, weedy relatives include ground ivy *(Glecoma hederacea)* and henbit *(Lamium amplexicaule)*.

Leguminosae

Legumes we eat include peas, and vetches and clovers are often used as cover crops or pasture plants. Black medic *(Medicago lupulina)* is a close relative.

Liliaceae

The bulb family includes onions, lilies, and most other flowers grown from true bulbs, as well as wild garlic *(Allium vineale)* and other wild onions. The prickly greenbriers *(Smilax* species) are members of the lily family, too.

Malvaceae

The mallow family includes hibiscus, hollyhocks, and okra, as well as these weeds:

- Mallow, *Malva neglecta*
- Prickly sida, *Sida spinosa*
- Velvetleaf, *Abutilon theophrasti*

Oxalidaceae

The oxalis family includes several ornamental flowers as well as yellow woodsorrel *(Oxalis stricta)*.

Phytolaccaceae

This small family includes pokeweed, *Phytolacca americana*.

Plantaginaceae

The plantains *(Plantago* species) have few close cousins.

Polygonaceae

The buckwheat family includes buckwheat, of course, along with several formidable weeds:

- Wild buckwheat, *Polygonum convolvulus*
- Docks, *Rumex* species
- Sorrel, *Rumex acetosella*

Portulacaceae

The Portulacas include the cultivated flower known as portulaca or moss rose and the widespread weed called purslane, *Portulaca oleracea.*

Ranunculaceae

Despite the common family name of crowfoot, most members of this family are pretty, including larkspurs, delphiniums, and ranunculus, along with weedy buttercups *(Ranunculus* species).

Rosaceae

The huge rose family includes many of our most beautiful flowers and delicious fruits, such as roses, apples, and strawberries. Weedy relations include the cinquefoils *(Potentilla* species).

Solanaceae

The robust nightshade family includes potatoes, tomatoes, peppers, and eggplant, as well as this rowdy group of weeds:

- Horsenettle, *Solanum carolinense*
- Jimsonweed, *Datura stramonium*
- Nightshades, *Solanum* species

Umbelliferae

This large and diverse group includes carrots, parsley, and several culinary herbs, along with the wildflower known as Queen Anne's lace and the poison hemlocks *(Cicuta maculata* and *Conium maculatum).*

Urticaceae

The small nettle family includes the stinging nettles, *Urtica* species.

◄ BIBLIOGRAPHY ►

All About Weeds, Edwin Rollins Spencer, Dover Publications, New York, 1957.

Common Weeds of the United States, Agricultural Research Service of the United States Department of Agriculture, Dover Publications, New York, 1971.

Identifying Seedling & Mature Weeds Common in the Southeastern United States, Jon M. Stucky, Thomas J. Monaco, and A.D. Worsham, North Carolina Agricultural Research Service and the North Carolina Cooperative Extension Service, North Carolina State University, Raleigh, NC, 1994.

"Intriguing World of Weeds," article series by Larry W. Mitich, which appeared in *Weeds Today* and *Weed Technology* from 1978 to 1992. A subject index of the series can be found in *Weed Technology*, Volume 5, page 916-918, 1991.

Weed Biology and Control, Thomas J. Muzik, McGraw-Hill, 1970.

Weed Identification and Control, Duane Isely, Iowa State University Press, Ames, IA, 1960.

Weed Physiology, Volume I, Reproduction and Ecophysiology, Stephen O. Duke, Editor, CRC Press, Inc., Boca Raton, FL, 1985. 3rd printing 1987.

Weeds, Walter Conrad Muenscher, Comstock Publishing, Cornell University Press, 2nd Edition, 1987.

Weeds, Control Without Poisons, Charles Walter, Jr., Acres U.S.A., Kansas City, MO, 1991.

Weeds, Guardians of the Soil, Joseph A. Cocannouer, Devin-Adair Co., New York, 1950.

Weeds of Colorado, Robert L. Zimdahl, Bulletin 521, Cooperative Extension, Colorado State University, Fort Collins, CO, 1983 edition, printed 1990.

Weeds of Lawn and Garden, John M. Fogg, Jr., University of Pennsylvania Press, Philadelphia, 1945.

Weeds of the North Central States, North Central Regional Research Publication No. 281, Bulletin 772, University of Illinois at Urbana-Champaign, College of Agriculture, Agricultural Experiment Station, 1981.

INDEX

Note: *italicized* page numbers refer to illustrations.

Blowball. *See* Dandelion

Bluebells of Scotland. *See* Bellflower, creeping

Bluegrass, annual *(Poa annua),* 7, 148, *149,* 191

Boards, used to control weeds, 20, *20*

Bottle grass. *See* Foxtail, green

Bristle grass. *See* Foxtail

Buckwheat, wild *(Polygonum convolvulus),* 176, *177,* 192

Bullbrier. *See* Greenbrier

Bull nettle. *See* Horsenettle

Buttercup, 192
    creeping *(Ranunculus repens),* 36–37, *38*
    tall *(Ranunculus acris),* 36–37, *39*

Butter flower/rose. *See* Buttercup

Butter print/weed. *See* Velvetleaf

Button bur. *See* Cocklebur

Buttonweed, Virginia *(Diodia virginiana),* 40, *41*

C

Cabbage looper, 97

Cabbageworm, 97

Campanulaceae family, 189

Canada thistle. *See* Thistle, Canada

Cancer root. *See* Pokeweed

Cankerwort. *See* Dandelion

Careless weed. *See* Pigweed

Carolina geranium. *See* Geranium, Carolina

Carolina nettle. *See* Horsenettle

Carpetweed *(Mollugo verticillata),* 48, *49,* 189

Caryophyllaceae family, 190

Case weed. *See* Shepherd's purse

Catbrier. *See* Greenbrier

Cat's foot. *See* Ivy, ground

Charlock. *See* Mustard

Cheeseweed. *See* Mallow

Chenopodiaceae family, 190

Chickens, used to control weeds, 20

Chickweed *(Stellaria media),* 7, 50, *51,* 52–53, 190

Chickweed, Indian/whorled. *See* Carpetweed

Chickweed, mouse-ear *(Cerastium vulgatum),* 52, 190

Chick wittles. *See* Chickweed

Chufa. *See* Nutsedge

Cinquefoil, 192
    oldfield *(Potentilla simplex),* 54–55, *55*
    rough *(Potentilla norvegica),* 54–55, *56*

Clotbur. *See* Cocklebur

Clover, black/hop. *See* Medic, black

Clover, subterranean *(Trifolium subterraneum),* 14–15

Clucken wort. *See* Chickweed

Cocklebur *(Xanthium pennsylvanicum, X. strumarium),* 5, 57–58, *59,* 190

Cocksfoot panicum. *See* Barnyardgrass

Cockspur grass. *See* Barnyardgrass

Coco sedge. *See* Nutsedge

Colewort. *See* Sowthistle

Colorado potato beetle, 83, 97

Compass plant. *See* Lettuce

Compositae family, 190

Controlling weeds
    methods for, 13–20
    tips for, 23–27

Convolvulaceae family, 190

Cornbind. *See* Buckwheat, wild

Cottonweed. *See* Milkweed; Velvetleaf

Couchgrass. *See* Quackgrass

Cover crops, use of, 13–15

Cowbane. *See* Hemlock, water

Crabgrass, 7, 9, 10, 191
    hairy *(Digitaria sanguinalis),* 155–56, *157*

Crabgrass *(continued)*
    smooth *(Digitaria ischaemum)*, 155–56, *158*
Cranesbill *(Geranium maculatum)*, 46
Creeping bellflower. *See* Bellflower, creeping
Creeping Charlie. *See* Ivy, ground
Creeping harebell. *See* Bellflower, creeping
Creeping jenny. *See* Bindweed
Creeping thistle. *See* Thistle, Canada
Creeping wheat. *See* Quackgrass
Crop mimicry, 8–9
Crowberry. *See* Pokeweed
Crowfoot. *See* Buttercup
Crowfoot grass. *See* Crabgrass
Crow garlic. *See* Garlic, wild
Crown vetch *(Coronilla varia)*, 21
Cruciferae family, 190
Cucold. *See* Spanishneedles
Cyperaceae family, 190

D

Daisy, oxeye *(Chrysanthemum leucanthemum)*, 22
Dandelion *(Taraxacum officinale)*, 5, 7, 62, *63*, 64, 190
Deadly nightshade. *See* Nightshade
Dead nettle. *See* Henbit
Devil grass. *See* Bermudagrass
Devil's grip. *See* Carpetweed
Devil's hair. *See* Dodder
Devil's potato. *See* Horsenettle
Devil's tomato. *See* Horsenettle
Disposal of weeds, 31–32
Ditch bur. *See* Cocklebur
Dock, 11, 192
    broadleaf *(Rumex obtusifolius)*, 65–66, *68*
    curly *(Rumex crispus)*, 65–66, *67*
    pale *(Rumex altissimus)*, 65–66, *69*

Dodder *(Cuscuta* species), 178, *179*, 190
Dogs-tooth-grass. *See* Bermudagrass
Dollar plant. *See* Ivy, ground

E

Earth almond. *See* Nutsedge
Edible galingale. *See* Nutsedge
Egyptian grass. *See* Johnsongrass
Euphorbiaceae family, 190
Eye-bright. *See* Spurge

F

False guinea grass. *See* Johnsongrass
Families of weeds, described, 189–92
Fat hen. *See* Lambsquarters
Field balm. *See* Ivy, ground
Field garlic. *See* Garlic, wild
Field kale. *See* Mustard
Finger grass. *See* Crabgrass
Five fingers. *See* Cinquefoil
Flea beetle, 83
Foxtail, 191
    giant *(Setaria faberi)*, 10, 160, *161*, 162
    green *(Setaria viridis)*, 160, *161*, 162
    yellow *(Setaria glauca)*, 160, *161*, 162
Frenchweed. *See* Galinsoga
Frost-blite. *See* Lambsquarters

G

Galingale, edible. *See* Nutsedge
Galinsoga *(Galinsoga ciliata)*, 70, *71*, 190
Garden berry. *See* Nightshade
Garlic, wild *(Allium vineale)*, 6, 8, 72, *73*, 74, 191
Geese, used to control weeds, 20
Geraniaceae family, 191
Geranium, Carolina *(Geranium carolinianum)*, 7, 46, *47*, 191
Gill-over-the-ground. *See* Ivy, ground

Sorrel *(Rumex acetosella)*, 7, 66, 128–29, *129*, 192
Sourgrass. *See* Woodsorrel
Sowthistle, 190
  annual *(Sonchus oleraceus, S. asper)*, 130–31, *132*
  perennial *(Sonchus arvensis)*, 130–31, *133*
Spanishneedles *(Bidens bipinnata)*, 134, *135*, 190
Spear-grass, annual/dwarf. *See* Bluegrass, annual
Spurge, 190
  family, 138
  prostrate *(Euphorbia supina)*, 10, 136, *137*
  spotted *(Euphorbia maculata)*, 136, *139*
Starweed. *See* Chickweed
Starwort. *See* Chickweed
Stinkwort. *See* Jimsonweed
Stitchwort. *See* Chickweed
Strawberry, barren. *See* Cinquefoil, oldfield

T

Tansy *(Tanacetum vulgare)*, 22
Tansy, wild. *See* Ragweed
Thistle, Canada *(Cirsium arvense)*, 5, 6, 10, 43–44, *45*, 190
Thorn-apple. *See* Jimsonweed
Toadflax *(Linaria vulgaris)*, 23

Tomato, nightshade and, 100, 101
Tomato, wild. *See* Horsenettle
Tomato viruses, 83
Tongue grass. *See* Chickweed; Pepperweed
Tools for weeding, 28–30, *29*, *30*
Trefoil, yellow. *See* Medic, black
Trumpet creeper *(Campsis radicans)*, 23

U

Umbelliferae family, 192
Urticaceae family, 192

V

Velvetleaf *(Abutilon theophrasti)*, 10, 142, *143*, 191
Violets *(Viola papillionacea)*, 23

W

Watergrass. *See* Barnyardgrass
White goosefoot. *See* Lambsquarters
Whorled chickweed. *See* Carpetweed
Winter-weed. *See* Chickweed
Wiregrass. *See* Bermudagrass
Woodbine. *See* Bindweed
Woodsorrel *(Oxalis stricta)*, 144, *145*, 191

Y

Yarrow *(Achillea millefolium; A. filipendulina)*, 23
Yellow trefoil. *See* Medic, black